OCT 2 1 2005

I0667051

RY

DISCARD

ETHELBERT B. CRAWFORD PUBLIC LIBRARY
393 BROADWAY, MONTICELLO, NY 12701

EQUAL JUSTICE UNDER LAW

The Pentagon Papers:
NATIONAL SECURITY OR
THE RIGHT TO KNOW

UNDER·LAW

SUPREME COURT MILESTONES

The Pentagon Papers:

NATIONAL SECURITY OR THE RIGHT TO KNOW

SUSAN DUDLEY GOLD

BENCHMARK BOOKS

MARSHALL CAVENDISH
NEW YORK

In memory of Margaret "Peg" Welch, local reporter and editor at the *Journal Tribune* in Biddeford, Maine, whose skill, intelligence, knowledge, and ethics guided us all

With special thanks to Professor David M. O'Brien of the Woodrow Wilson Department of Politics at the University of Virginia for reviewing the text of this book, and to the Rev. Raymond Hopkins for sharing his keen observations and memories of his role in the Pentagon Papers case.

Benchmark Books • Marshall Cavendish • 99 White Plains Road Tarrytown, NY 10591 • www.marshallcavendish.com • Copyright © 2005 by Susan Dudley Gold • All rights reserved. No part of this book may be reproduced or utilized in any form or by any means electronic or mechanical including photocopying, recording, or by any information storage and retrieval system, without permission from the copyright holders.

All Internet sites were available and accurate when sent to press.

Library of Congress Cataloging-in-Publication Data Gold, Susan Dudley. • The Pentagon papers : national security or the right to know / by Susan Dudley Gold.
p. cm. • Includes bibliographical references and index. • ISBN 0-7614-1843-1
1. New York Times Company—Trials, litigation, etc.—Juvenile literature. 2. Pentagon Papers—Juvenile literature. 3. Security classification (Government documents)—United States—Juvenile literature. 4. Freedom of the press—United States—Juvenile literature. 5. Vietnamese Conflict, 1961-1975—United States—Juvenile literature. I. Title.
KF228.N52G65 2004 • 342.7308'53—dc22 • 2004008583

Photo Research by Candlepants Incorporated

Cover Photo: Copyright © Royalty-Free Corbis

The photographs in this book are used by permission and through the courtesy of: *Corbis*: Royalty Free. 2–3, Bettmann, 6, 11, 13, 19, 21, 22, 44, 100, 102, 115; Corbis, 43, 65, 84, 86; Ramin Talaie, 107; *Collection of the Supreme Court of the United States*: 28, 32; AP/Wide World Photos: *48, 52, 56;* New York Times: *Barton Silverman, 50; Edward Hausner, 93;* The Washington Post, reprinted with permission. Photo by Charles Del Vecchio: *85.*

Series design by Sonia Chaghatzbanian
Printed in China
1 3 5 6 4 2

contents

DANIEL ELLSBERG, WHO LEAKED PORTIONS OF THE PENTAGON PAPERS TO THE PRESS,
TESTIFIES AT A CONGRESSIONAL HEARING ON THE VIETNAM WAR IN JULY 1971.

INTRODUCTION

AMENDMENT I TO THE U.S. CONSTITUTION

Congress shall make no law respecting an establishment of religion, or prohibiting the free exercise thereof; or abridging the freedom of speech, or of the press; or the right of the people peaceably to assemble, and to petition the Government for a redress of grievances.

ON SUNDAY, JUNE 13, 1971, The New York Times published the first of a ten-part series of articles and accompanying top secret government documents that were part of what would become known as the Pentagon Papers.

The full Pentagon Papers, a secret history of U.S. involvement in Vietnam from 1945 to 1968, filled forty-seven volumes. Shortly after the series began, the U.S. government sought and won a court order to stop the *Times* from publishing any more of the top secret documents. As soon as the *Times* stopped publishing the Pentagon Papers, the *Washington Post* began its own series on the documents. It, too, was forced to stop publishing the reports after the government won a temporary court-ordered ban.

The Pentagon Papers revealed the government's "contempt for public opinion," its use of the press to mislead the public, and "the easy arrogance" of leaders who made decisions without the knowledge or consent of the people or Congress, according to a *Washington Post* editorial.

For the first time in history, the U.S. government went to court to stop newspapers from printing a story officials said threatened the nation's security. This demand for "prior restraint"—preventing an article from being printed—led almost immediately to court. Within days the two cases—involving the *Times* and the *Post*— were heard as one before the Supreme Court on an emergency expedited basis.

The government's lawyers said the *Times* and other newspapers were guilty of treason and had endangered the lives of U.S. soldiers fighting a war by printing the Pentagon Papers. The U.S. Constitution, they argued, gave the president the power to conduct foreign affairs and command the military. This in turn gave him the authority to censor the press to protect national security.

The newspapers argued that the First Amendment to the Constitution protects freedom of the press. Government review or censorship of information has a chilling effect on the public's right to know. Only under the most dire circumstances—not present in this case—could the government stop the presses, they argued.

The drama that unfolded as a result of the landmark cases—*New York Times* v. *United States* and *United States* v. *Washington Post*—confirmed the vital role a free press plays in American democracy.

The publication of the Pentagon Papers that followed the decision uncovered a longstanding pattern of secrecy and lies that government officials had used to protect themselves from criticism. But few people read more than excerpts of the 7,000-page study. The revelations about U.S. actions in Vietnam had little immediate impact on government policy. The controversy over the study, however, indirectly led to President Richard M. Nixon's resignation and, ultimately, to U.S. withdrawal from Vietnam.

one
THE PENTAGON STUDY

THE STEADY WHIR OF A COPY MACHINE seemed louder than it was in the quiet of the deserted office. A slim, nervous man stood over the machine, methodically placing one sheet after another on top of the copier's smooth surface. His serious, dark eyes watched as the pages collected in the tray. He worked late into the night, gathering the copies, collating them, and reassembling the originals. Before dawn, he stuffed the sets of papers—copies and originals—into a briefcase, locked up the office, and walked into the warm California air of early autumn.

Before his colleagues reported to work, he slipped through the security checkpoint at Rand Corporation, a Santa Monica think tank where he worked as a government consultant. The guard knew him, nodded his usual good morning, and paid little attention to the bulging briefcase the man carried. Once in the Rand offices, the man returned the original documents to the company's safe. That evening, he would take another set of papers past the guard and follow the same routine. Week after week, he worked by day and copied by night until he had reproduced the entire forty-seven volumes—3,000 pages of documents and 4,000 pages of analysis—of what would become known as the Pentagon Papers.

Daniel Ellsberg had faced enemy guns on combat patrols in Vietnam. He had served in the Marine Corps and worked at the Pentagon. His clandestine visits to the copy machine, however, exposed him to threats from the most powerful forces in the world—the U.S. presidency and the American court system. His actions also brought him worldwide fame as the man who leaked the Pentagon Papers.

VIETNAM QUAGMIRE

Like the rest of the country, Ellsberg had watched the United States become mired in a war in Vietnam that seemed to have no end. By the late 1960s many Americans had had enough. Thousands of protesters clamored for the withdrawal of U.S. troops. President Lyndon B. Johnson had decided in March 1968 not to run for reelection in the wake of severe criticism over his handling of the war. Violent protests in Chicago had disrupted the Democratic National Convention later that summer. Disgusted voters turned away from the Democratic candidate, Hubert H. Humphrey, who, as Johnson's vice president, carried the stigma of the war even as he pledged to end it.

After winning in a close race, Republican Richard M. Nixon took the oath of office in January 1969. Despite his promise to work for peace, Nixon had continued the same bombing strategies that presidents before him had followed. Nixon's national security adviser, Henry Kissinger, had begun secret negotiations with the North Vietnamese, but Ellsberg and others feared the president would order more bombing raids to force the enemy to agree to U.S. terms.

Ellsberg, a brilliant analyst who had been a student of Kissinger's at Harvard University, gradually came to oppose the war. In 1967, Ellsberg had worked on a small portion of a massive study on U.S. involvement in Vietnam that had been ordered by then-Defense Secretary Robert S. McNamara. Titled "History of U.S. Decision-Making Process on Vietnam Policy," the report detailed America's actions in the region dating back to 1945. McNamara served as secretary of defense during the Kennedy and Johnson administrations. An early proponent of the

DEFENSE SECRETARY ROBERT McNAMARA POINTS TO A MAP OF VIETNAM AS HE DESCRIBES AN ATTACK BY U.S. AIRCRAFT UNDER WAY IN 1964 AGAINST TORPEDO BOAT BASES AND INSTALLATIONS.

Vietnam War, he believed, as many others did at the time, that the United States had to take a stand in Southeast Asia or risk losing the entire area to communist Russian control. If the area fell under communist control, many Americans believed, it would weaken the West and increase the threat of a nuclear war between the two superpowers. This line of thinking—dubbed the domino theory—controlled U.S. foreign policy in the region for three decades. It underscored the militaristic tension between the United States and Russia (then-Soviet Union) during this period, known as the Cold War.

McNamara supported President John F. Kennedy's policies in South Vietnam and later, President Johnson's decision, in early February 1965, to bomb North Vietnam and to send U.S. troops to the region. By mid-1965, however, the secretary of defense began questioning whether the United States could succeed in Vietnam. He advised

Johnson to stop the bombing and negotiate a peace settlement with North Vietnam. Johnson did so in December 1965, but the peace talks failed and the bombing resumed.

As the war dragged on, McNamara became convinced that America was following the wrong course in Vietnam. Each administration beginning with Harry S. Truman had used tactics that repeatedly failed to achieve America's goals in Southeast Asia. U.S. policy had been to threaten more bombing—and then do it—as a way of strengthening America's position in peace negotiations. But the strategy had not worked and, McNamara was convinced, would not work. In fact, it had the effect of extending the war.

The defense secretary believed that the best path to peace was to accept North Vietnam's terms and withdraw from the country. "We were wrong, terribly wrong," McNamara wrote about America's Vietnam policy in a 1995 confessional book, *In Retrospect*, which detailed the Vietnam decisions of the Kennedy and Johnson era.

McNamara's views in 1965 that the United States should stop the bombing, cut back troops, and work quickly to negotiate a settlement put him at odds with Johnson and others in the administration. In 1968 he left his defense post to become president of the World Bank.

PRESERVING HISTORY

While still secretary of defense, McNamara asked John McNaughton, his assistant secretary, to collect documents relating to America's involvement in Vietnam. McNamara later said he wanted to ensure that future generations got an accurate picture of what happened in Vietnam. Preserving the documents, he believed, would allow Americans to assess the conflict for themselves and benefit from the lessons of Vietnam.

"In 1965 and 1966," McNamara said in a 1975 interview, "I believed that the decisions that were being taken

THE INAUGURATION CEREMONY OF RICHARD M. NIXON ON JANUARY 20, 1969.

were so momentous with respect to the history of our
nation that it was essential we preserve the records of the
day that related to them . . . so that future historians would
have access to them, could reappraise the decisions, and
draw lessons from them."

After issuing the order for the report, McNamara
turned the project completely over to his aides. Because
he was a key figure in the events being studied, he did not
want to be involved in the report in any way. As it turned
out, the Pentagon Papers, McNamara later acknowledged,
"didn't take quite the form I had in mind when we started
the project." But, he said, the study and the controversies
that later developed confirmed "my concern that documents and records of the time be preserved and made
available for later study and evaluation by historians."

Some observers believe that if McNamara had not commissioned the report, many of the papers documenting U.S. actions, policies, and strategies would have been destroyed by political leaders intent on protecting their reputations.

When John McNaughton died in a plane crash shortly after the project began, Morton H. Halperin, Leslie H. Gelb, and Paul C. Warnke undertook the massive job. All three worked at the Defense Department. Warnke had assumed McNaughton's post as assistant secretary of defense after the latter's death. McNamara had ordered that the project be kept secret, so few people knew of the team's activities.

The Pentagon Papers study, ordered by McNamara in June 1967, eventually covered United States-Vietnam relations from 1945 to 1968. Besides the original documents that McNamara had requested, it included reports that analyzed U.S. actions and policy. The final forty-seven-volume report included four volumes of documents and analyses of U.S. diplomatic policies from 1964 to 1968. These last four volumes contained especially sensitive background material developed for use during negotiations with North Vietnam.

The team compiling the study finished it just days before Richard Nixon's inauguration as president of the United States in January 1969. Neither Johnson nor Nixon knew of the existence of the secret study until parts of it appeared in *The New York Times*.

TWO
THE LEAK

WHEN CHIEF JUSTICE EARL WARREN administered the oath of office to Richard M. Nixon, the president-elect pledged to "consecrate my office, my energies, and all the wisdom I can summon, to the cause of peace among nations."

War, however, continued to play a headline role in America. Even as Nixon prepared to assume the presidency, demonstrations by antiwar protesters delayed the inaugural parade down Pennsylvania Avenue to the Capitol Building. The Tet Offensive the previous January had seriously undermined the American public's will to continue the war. During that attack, on the Vietnamese New Year's holiday (Tet), North Vietnam forces launched a massive assault on more than one hundred cities and U.S. bases in South Vietnam. There were thousands of deaths—mostly among the northern troops and their allies.

The communist forces had hoped the Tet attacks would lead to an uprising among the South Vietnamese people against their government. That did not happen, and ultimately the communist forces in the south were decimated. Before they were defeated, however, television crews broadcast the communists' initial success in reaching the U.S. embassy in Saigon, the South Vietnamese capital.

Even before the offensive, polls showed that more Americans opposed the war than favored it. Heavy television news coverage of the Tet attacks belied President Johnson's assertion that the war was winding down. In the end, even though the communists failed militarily, their offensive turned a war-weary American public against further U.S. involvement. Unsettled by the Tet reports, members of Congress and other public officials added their criticisms of American policy in Vietnam.

In early March 1968, *The New York Times* reported that General William Westmoreland, the U.S. commander in Vietnam, had asked for more than 200,000 additional troops. This provided even more ammunition to those calling for America to get out of Vietnam. On March 31, President Johnson made his surprising announcement that he would not run for reelection and that he would stop the bombing in North Vietnam and seek to negotiate a peace settlement.

Shortly after Nixon took office, Kissinger hired Rand Corporation to develop possible Vietnam strategies. Daniel Ellsberg, one of the consultants who worked on the report, advised against further bombing. Among the strategies he suggested was to withdraw U.S. troops from Vietnam. By 1969, more than 550,000 American soldiers were serving there. Kissinger would later omit any reference to withdrawal from the final report.

During this time, Nixon—like Johnson before him—used the threat of more bombing to add force to U.S. demands during peace negotiations. "He was making such threats and then he was prepared to carry them out," Ellsberg said later in an interview.

Ellsberg became convinced that Nixon would escalate the war. The consultant knew that two copies of the top secret Pentagon Papers on which he had worked were stored in the Rand Corporation safe. He asked to be allowed to read the entire 7,000-page study. Since he had top-security clearance and was working on a Pentagon project at the time, Ellsberg won permission to view the papers.

convincing evidence against war

What he read in the Pentagon Papers convinced Ellsberg that continuing the war was wrong. The report revealed that U.S. presidents and government officials had continually lied to the public about American policy and its chances of success. In a key passage, Ellsberg read that Johnson had sent more troops to Vietnam while telling the American public that he had no plans to expand the war. Other sections showed that U.S. officials did not believe America could win the war in Vietnam. Even so, and despite advice to the contrary, every president starting with Truman had insisted on continuing U.S. involvement in Vietnam. They prolonged the war because no president had the political will to admit defeat and withdraw. Ellsberg concluded that Nixon would be no different.

"The fact now that Nixon was embarked on a new course held out very little hope that he would be more responsive just to good advice about getting out than any of his predecessors had been," Ellsberg said later.

For several months, Ellsberg had grown increasingly opposed to the war in Vietnam. He attended peace rallies. He talked with a young protester named Randall Kehler, who chose to go to jail rather than serve in what he considered to be an immoral war. The conversation revealed to Ellsberg that "there were other ways of being conscientious than serving the president." For several weeks, Anthony J. Russo Jr., Ellsberg's friend and coworker at Rand, briefed him on a project Russo had done on the Viet Cong's motivation and morale. The Viet Cong were South Vietnam forces fighting with the North Vietnamese. The results of his study had led Russo to oppose the war. Ellsberg, too, came to believe that the war was unjust and tantamount to "mass murder."

In September 1969, the U.S. Army dropped murder charges against Colonel Robert Rheault, a U.S. commander of special forces in Vietnam who had been accused of killing a Vietnamese civilian. The government's handling of the case and comments made about the war—which Ellsberg knew to be lies because of what he had read in the Pentagon Papers—enraged him. Ellsberg decided he had to find a way to make the documents public.

"It occurred to me," he wrote in his 2002 book, *Secrets: A Memoir of Vietnam and the Pentagon Papers*, "that what I had in my safe at Rand was seven thousand pages of documentary evidence of lying, by four presidents and their administrations over twenty-three years, to conceal plans and actions of mass murder. I decided I would stop concealing that myself. I would get it out somehow."

Ellsberg believed that Americans should read the study and learn for themselves of the government's deceit. He hoped that the resulting public outrage would force the Nixon administration to end the war once and for all. Russo urged Ellsberg to make the papers public. He also arranged for Ellsberg to copy the study at Russo's girlfriend's advertising agency. For the next few weeks Ellsberg or Russo spent their nights copying the Pentagon Papers.

No Takers

Ellsberg originally planned to leak the Pentagon Papers to Congress. He believed the Pentagon study would push Congress into holding hearings on how the war was being conducted. And the hearings, he hoped, would uncover Nixon's plans to extend the war. Ellsberg believed that when the public heard the truth, they would pressure Congress to end the war.

In November 1969, he offered the papers to Senator J. William Fulbright, chair of the Senate Foreign Relations Committee. Fulbright read portions of the study and later asked the federal government to release the documents to Congress. The administration refused Fulbright's repeated requests to do so.

During this time, Ellsberg copied other top secret papers used in compiling the Pentagon Papers. Among these was a

IN 1969, DANIEL ELLSBERG OFFERED TO RELEASE THE PENTAGON PAPERS TO SENATOR J. WILLIAM FULBRIGHT (D-ARKANSAS). FULBRIGHT URGED THE NIXON ADMINISTRATION TO RELEASE THE STUDY TO CONGRESS, BUT THE PRESIDENT REFUSED TO DO SO.

report on the Tonkin Gulf affair in August 1964. Back then, U.S. officials had reported that North Vietnamese torpedo boats had launched two "unprovoked attacks" on American ships in the Tonkin Gulf. President Johnson used the incident to gain Congressional approval of the Gulf of Tonkin Resolution to wage full-scale war in Vietnam. Later evidence, however, showed that the first attack was in response to U.S. spy activities and the second attack never occurred.

For the next several months, Ellsberg tried to interest other members of Congress, including Senator George McGovern, in the study. No one seemed interested in making the papers public. He even spoke with Kissinger about the papers, urging the national security adviser to read them. Kissinger reportedly discounted their importance. Ellsberg also gave parts of the Pentagon report to Marcus G. Raskin and Richard J. Barnet of the Institute for Policy Studies. They used portions of the report in their book on the Vietnam War, *Washington Plans an Aggressive War*, published in 1971.

In the spring of 1970, Ellsberg accepted a position with the Massachusetts Institute of Technology and moved to Cambridge, Massachusetts, near Boston. He brought the copies of the Pentagon Papers with him when he moved.

Nixon continued to escalate the war. On Nixon's orders, U.S. bombers attacked Cambodia, then Laos. Ellsberg was becoming desperate in his attempts to make the Pentagon Papers public.

A RIGHT TO KNOW

Finally, in early 1971, Ellsberg decided the only way the American people would learn about the Pentagon Papers was to release them to the press. He called *New York Times* reporter Neil Sheehan. Ellsberg believed the *Times* was the only newspaper that would print the original documents as well as articles on the Pentagon Papers. Publishing the documents was crucial, Ellsberg thought, because without them, the American public might not believe the reporters' stories. "When it comes to contradicting the president and alerting the public to a situation which [endangers] the national security and many human lives . . . there is no substitute for documents," Ellsberg said.

The two men met several times in February and March to discuss the papers. Ellsberg had first met Sheehan in Vietnam, where the reporter covered the war as a *Times* correspondent and a bureau chief for United Press International. He later was assigned to Washington, D.C., where he reported on the Johnson and Nixon administrations.

Sheehan has never fully explained how he got the Pentagon Papers. According to Ellsberg, he did not personally hand Sheehan the papers or come to a final agreement on how they would be used. But Ellsberg did give the reporter a key to the Cambridge apartment where he had stored the papers. Sometime near the middle of March, Sheehan went to the empty apartment, took the papers, photocopied them, and returned them to their hiding place, according to Ellsberg's account.

By not handing the top secret papers directly to Sheehan, Ellsberg hoped to avoid criminal prosecution. Ellsberg much preferred giving the documents to a member of Congress because he believed constitutional protections guaranteed to Congress members would help shield him as well. But he had to scrap that plan when no one in Congress seemed willing to make the documents public.

Leaking the documents to the press was riskier. Ellsberg knew that his actions might very well land him in jail. But it

In 1965, troops of the U.S. Army 1st Brigade Infantry, a search-and-destroy operation south of Bien Hoa Airbase, stop to eat C-ration food. Missions such as these were detailed in the Pentagon Papers.

was a risk he was willing to take. As a civilian liaison officer, he had faced death in Vietnam when he believed in the war. He now felt a responsibility to reveal the truth about that war. "If I was willing to be blown up in Vietnam or captured, as friends of mine were, when I accepted the cause or supported it, should I not be willing to go to prison or risk my freedom?" Ellsberg asked in a 1998 interview. "And when I faced that question, it was quickly answered." The decision would later lead to his arrest and the end of his career as a government consultant. It would also link his name forever with the cause of freedom of the press and the public's right to know.

The four volumes on negotiations with the North Vietnamese were not among the papers leaked to the press or to Congress. These documents were not released until 1977 when the government lifted their top secret classification.

DRIVEN FROM THEIR HOMES DURING HEAVY FIGHTING IN 1968, SOUTH VIETNAMESE REFUGEES CROUCH UNDER A TREE WHILE AN AMERICAN SOLDIER GUARDS THEM.

Sheehan said later that he made a "personal decision that [the report] belonged in the public domain." The documents, he said, were public property and would enlighten the public about "one of the most traumatic experiences" in the country's history. The Pentagon Papers were "paid for by the people of this country with 50,000 lives and nearly a hundred billion dollars and . . . they had a right to know this information."

With documents in hand, Sheehan went to his editors at *The New York Times*. He argued convincingly that the documents were genuine and that the *Times* should publish them. *Times* officials were not yet ready to make such a momentous decision, but they told Sheehan to study the papers and prepare a report. Sheehan carried out his top secret work in a room at the Jefferson Hotel in Washington, D.C. Later, a fifty-person team of reporters working on the story moved the operation to the New York Hilton. The project was so secret they didn't dare to work at the *Times* offices for fear government officials or other media would learn of the story.

THree
PRIOR RESTRAINT:
CENSORSHIP VERSUS CENSURE

FreeDOM OF THE Press has long been a cornerstone of American and English law. Since the end of the seventeenth century, the people of these two nations have opposed government censorship of the press. Banning items *before* they are published—prior restraint—has been seen by the people as being at odds with a free society. In almost all cases, longstanding English and American law prevents governments from stopping the presses.

On the other hand, people (and firms) may be punished *after* publication if the material is libelous or pornographic. And they may be stopped from publishing the material again.

For centuries, kings, governments, and church officials have tried to control what could be printed. In 1501, only about fifty years after Johannes Gutenberg introduced printing to the world, Pope Alexander VI issued orders that all material had to be approved by the church before publication. After unapproved pamphlets began circulating in England, King Henry VIII in 1534 ordered all English printing presses to be licensed. Printers could not publish anything that had not first been cleared by the state. When English poet John Milton published a pamphlet in 1644 defending the right to divorce, officials threatened to prosecute him for printing without a license. In response, Milton wrote *Areopagitica*, an ardent defense of freedom of the press. Others took up the battle, and in 1695 Parliament abolished press licensing laws.

Sir William Blackstone, the foremost eighteenth-century expert on English law, noted the crucial role of the press in a democracy. "The liberty of the press," he wrote, "is indeed essential to the nature of a free state." Blackstone echoed Milton's premise that the press should be free to publish whatever it pleased. But if "improper, mischievous or illegal" material were published, then those responsible justifiably faced punishment: "This [freedom of the press] consists in laying no previous restraints upon publications, and not in freedom from censure for criminal matter when published."

AMERICA'S PRESS: PROTECTING LIBERTY

The English colonists brought England's legal system—including a distaste for government censorship—with them when they settled in the New World. They also brought printing presses to America. In 1690, Benjamin Harris published the colonies' first newspaper, *Publick Occurrences Both Foreign and Domestick*, in Boston. The newspaper's articles so infuriated colonial officials that they shut it down after only one edition. John Campbell's *Boston News-Letter*, published in 1704, became the first successful newspaper in the colonies. Soon newspapers appeared throughout the region. By 1820, 582 newspapers were being published in America.

Peter Zenger began publishing the *New York Weekly Journal* in 1733. His stinging criticism of the colony's governor landed him in jail charged with libel. The law at the time allowed publishers to be arrested and punished for printing material that criticized certain people or governments, even if the information was true.

In a case that would set the foundation for press freedom in America, Zenger's lawyer argued in 1735 that because the journal had printed the truth, the charges could not be considered libelous. The jury agreed and freed Zenger.

The press soon led the charge against what colonists viewed as unjust English rule. When England passed the Stamp Act of 1765 taxing all newspapers, legal documents, and business papers used in the colonies, Samuel Adams printed flyers urging colonists to resist. The printed word—and the resultant revolt—proved stronger than England's will; the English Parliament repealed the act in 1766. A jubilant Adams proclaimed the power of the press:

"Your Press has sounded the alarm. . . . It has pointed to this people their danger and their remedy."

Thomas Paine's writings on England's tyranny— "These are the times that try men's souls"—helped spark the American Revolution. In his most famous piece, a pamphlet called *Common Sense*, Paine argued passionately for independence from Great Britain. The pamphlet, published in January 1776, sold more than 500,000 copies.

After the war, Thomas Jefferson and others pushed for a document that would protect citizens' individual rights, among them freedom of the press. As a result, the founders drew up the Bill of Rights, the first ten amendments to the U.S. Constitution, which were ratified in 1791. The First Amendment declared, among other things, that Congress could not make a law abridging the freedom of speech, or of the press.

The fact that freedom of the press appears in the First Amendment is an indication of its importance to those early American leaders. Jefferson particularly cherished the role newspapers played in protecting liberty. He expressed that view in 1787:

The basis of our government being the opinion of the people, the very first object should be to keep that right; and were it left to me to decide whether we should have a government without newspapers, or newspapers without a government, I should not hesitate a moment to prefer the latter.

In England and the United States, the press's role in government and society gained in importance. The British Parliament first allowed journalists to attend sessions in the late 1700s. By reporting on the activities of officials, the press served as a check on government's abuse of power. In doing that, the press stood as an unofficial guardian of freedom along with the three branches of government: the executive (the president in the United States), the legislature (U.S. Congress), and the judiciary (Supreme Court).

Edmund Burke is credited with first referring to the press as the Fourth Estate. In an address to the House of Commons in the late eighteenth century, he declared that the press was the "fourth estate [of the realm], more powerful than all the rest." That was not necessarily good, according to Burke. He noted that the press did not have to be capable or worthy to be heard: "It matters not what rank he has, what revenues or garnitures: the requisite thing is that he have a tongue which others will listen to; this and nothing more is requisite."

In modern-day America, Supreme Court Justice Potter Stewart, who served on the Court from 1958 to 1981, reaffirmed the notion that the press exists as a government watchdog—a role conferred by the First Amendment. In a 1974 speech, the justice said the "primary purpose" of the First Amendment was "to create a fourth institution outside the government as an additional check on the three official branches."

CENSORSHIP LAWS

Even with the First Amendment's guarantee, however, officials found ways to curb the publication of material critical of their administrations. In 1798 the Federalists passed a sweeping law to muzzle Republican critics, among them Thomas Jefferson. The Sedition Act of 1798 made it illegal for anyone to publish "any false, scandalous and malicious writings" against the government of the United States, Congress, or the president. Those who violated the law faced a fine and a jail sentence.

The Federalists argued that the law was needed because of attacks on U.S. merchant ships by mercenaries supported by the French Revolutionary government. The so-called Undeclared Naval War with France raged from 1798 to 1800. The Sedition Act expired in 1801, when Jefferson became president.

Wartime often pitted security-conscious officials against a news-hungry press. While most Americans opposed government censorship during peacetime, many worried that newspapers might print articles that would harm the country during war. Officials used that fear to win support for secrecy and press censorship.

Shortly after the United States entered World War I, Congress passed the Espionage Act of 1917. Like the Sedition Act of 1798, the law took aim at enemies within the United States. Supporters of the law, including President Woodrow Wilson, spoke of an America filled with spies, intrigue, and disloyal plotters. The original act contained a provision to censor the press, but it was omitted after critics protested that it violated the Constitution. Instead, the press was asked not to publish information on foreign affairs without first checking with the State Department. That part of the law was voluntary.

The following year, in 1918, Congress passed an amendment to the act, known as the Sedition Act. Its provisions reinstated censorship. Under the new law, Americans were barred from using "any disloyal, profane, scurrilous, or abusive language about the form of government . . . the Constitution . . . or the flag of the United States, or the uniform of the Army and Navy." The government used the law to ban books, newspapers, and journals.

Pacifists also became targets under the law. Eugene V. Debs, a socialist candidate for president in 1912, faced a ten-year jail sentence after speaking out against the war at a 1918 rally. His conviction was later upheld by the Supreme Court, but President Warren G. Harding pardoned him in 1921.

THE ISSUE OF FREE SPEECH VERSUS NATIONAL SECURITY WAS FIRST DEBATED LONG BEFORE THE PENTAGON PAPERS. JUSTICE OLIVER WENDELL HOLMES SET LIMITS ON FREE SPEECH IN THE 1919 CASE, *SCHENCK* V. *UNITED STATES.*

CULTURE OF SECRECY

The high Court upheld the Espionage Act and the Sedition Act in a 1919 case, *Schenck* v. *United States.* The case involved a pamphlet produced by Charles T. Schenck during World War I that claimed the military draft was illegal. Schenck was found guilty of violating the Espionage Act. The U.S. Supreme Court upheld the conviction.

Writing for the Court, Justice Oliver Wendell Holmes set limits on free speech. Words could be banned, Holmes wrote, if they created a "clear and present danger" to society, especially in wartime. Courts could also grant injunctions to prevent such speech, according to the opinion. Congress repealed the Sedition Act in 1920, but the Court ruling remained a standard used to judge free speech. Later decisions, however, would make it more difficult to censor material.

In the aftermath of World War II and the beginning of the Cold War, Congress passed another law related to security. The National Security Act of 1947 created the National Security Council and the Central Intelligence Agency (CIA) and put the armed forces under one department. As a result of the law, a vast bureaucracy emerged with secrecy as its lifeblood.

Frightened by Cold War threats, Americans accepted more restrictions. According to a 1997 Senate report on secrecy, such restrictions were "the awful dilemma" of the Cold War years: "To preserve an open society, it was deemed necessary to take measures that in significant ways closed it down." Government kept a lock on Cold War information, creating a culture of secrecy. Under the Atomic Energy Act of 1946, for example, some material automatically became top secret without officials ever having to classify it.

Another law, passed in 1946, attempted to pry open some government operations. The Administrative Procedure Act (APA) required government agencies to keep the public informed about their doings. However, the law exempted "any function of the United States requiring secrecy in the public interest." Specifically, this included operations involving the military and foreign affairs.

Leaks of classified military secrets in the 1950s caused grave concern among officials. They were already wary of the growing threat posed by the Soviet Union during the Cold War years. In an effort to plug the leaks and tighten security measures, Congress formed the Wright Commission to update the Espionage Act.

The commission issued its report in 1957. Its proposals to get government secrets under control took two routes. One was to cut back on the amount of material to be classified. Keeping information secret unnecessarily "retards scientific and technological progress," the commission noted.

The commission's second proposal took an opposite tack. It proposed expanding the espionage laws to cover all secret government documents and would have made it a crime for the press (or anyone else) to reveal such material. In the past, such laws had focused only on military documents given to foreign spies.

The proposal brought immediate protests from critics

who viewed it as prior restraint of the press. *New York Times* columnist James Reston took aim at the proposal when he described how newspapers often reveal classified information. In one such instance, he said, the *Times* published plans on the formation of the United Nations. Far from undermining the process as the U.S. government claimed it would, Reston said the *Times* article sparked a "long debate" that in turn "helped clarify" issues under discussion. "Under the legislation now proposed," Reston wrote, "it [the *Times* article] would have been a clear case for criminal action."

The proposal died when Congress failed to act on the commission's report. Under prodding from Representative John E. Moss, D-California, the focus of Congress began to shift from secrets to open government. In 1966, the Freedom of Information Act (FOIA) forced the door open by requiring agencies to make many records available to the public. Bureaucratic red tape and delays, however, made it difficult and time-consuming to see government records. The law was strengthened several times, most recently in 2000.

The passage of the FOIA marked major gains for the right of the public (and the press) to obtain information. However, the law exempted several categories of records, including those decreed by the president "to be kept secret in the interest of national defense or foreign policy."

The government would file suit against the newspapers in the Pentagon Papers case based on this passage and on the Espionage Act.

COURT CASES AND THE PRESS

The U.S. Supreme Court's first major ruling on freedom of the press came in a 1931 case called *Near* v. *Minnesota*. The case, in a narrow 5 to 4 ruling, severely limited the government's ability to put prior restraint on the press. It also upheld the right of the press to criticize public officials. This ruling would play a central role in the court battles over the Pentagon Papers.

The case involved a weekly newspaper called *The Saturday Press*, which published a series of articles in 1927 charging that "Jewish gangsters" ran gambling, bootlegging, and racketeering operations in Minneapolis. The articles also accused several local officials of abetting the crimes or knowing about illegal activity and taking no action to curb it. County attorney Floyd B. Olson, himself the target of *The Saturday Press*'s vicious barbs, sued Jay M. Near, the newspaper's publisher, and asked the court to stop further publication of the articles. Olson based his suit on a Minnesota law that banned publication of "a malicious, scandalous and defamatory newspaper, magazine or other periodical" as a public nuisance. The law allowed such publications only if the publisher could prove they were true and published "with good motives and for justifiable ends."

Ruling that the newspaper had indeed published "malicious, scandalous, and defamatory articles," the district court shut the paper down. Near appealed to the state supreme court. He argued that the state law was unconstitutional and violated both the First Amendment's guarantee of freedom of the press and the Fourteenth Amendment, which prevented states from depriving citizens of their liberties. A unanimous court rejected Near's claims.

The case reached the Supreme Court in 1931. In a landmark decision, the Court ruled in Near's favor. In strong words, Chief Justice Charles Evans Hughes confirmed the ban on prior restraint of the press in almost all cases. Under the Constitution, he wrote, except in very rare circumstances, the presses can't be stopped—not by courts, not even by public officials who have reason to believe that the material to be printed will target them unjustly.

Almost no attempts to stop the publication of articles critical of public officials had been made in the past one hundred and fifty years, according to Hughes. This indicated the "deep-seated conviction that such restraints would violate constitutional right," the justice wrote. In fact, Hughes noted, the "chief purpose" of the First Amendment's guarantee of press freedom is "to prevent previous restraints upon publication."

People who published false, scandalous items could be punished under libel laws, Hughes pointed out. But to silence the press beforehand—even when articles to be printed might be false and when publishers might be irresponsible—would threaten the very underpinning of a free nation.

Hughes wrote: "The fact that the liberty of the press may be abused by miscreant purveyors of scandal does not make any the less necessary the immunity of the press from previous restraint in dealing with official misconduct."

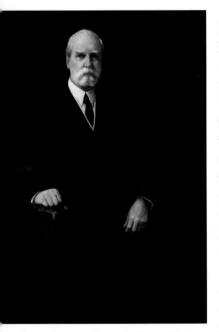

CHIEF JUSTICE CHARLES EVANS HUGHES ISSUED THE 1931 DECISION IN *NEAR* V. *MINNESOTA*, THE FIRST MAJOR RULING ON FREEDOM OF THE PRESS. HUGHES CONFIRMED THE BAN ON PRIOR RESTRAINT OF THE PRESS IN ALMOST ALL CASES.

The decision also attacked the Minnesota law's provision that a publisher could resume publishing if he could prove ahead of time that his statements were true and published "with good motives." Such a stipulation would mean that a publisher would be forced to get approval from officials to publish. The officials would then be in a position to approve for publication only material they agreed with. If this were allowed, Hughes noted, "it would be but a step to a complete system of censorship."

The chief justice outlined the few exceptional cases when the press could be restrained. When the nation is at war, he noted, the government could stop publications that would interfere with recruitment or reveal things like sailing dates of ships or the number and location of troops.

In defining the important role of the press in a free and open society, Hughes looked back at the Sedition Act of 1798. That law forbade articles critical of officials. If it still stood, Hughes asked, might not the United States "be miserable colonies, groaning under a foreign yoke?" Instead, the United States became a "free and independent nation," in large part, Hughes said, because of a free press. In America and beyond, a free press helped uncover corruption and governmental abuses. "To the press alone, chequered as it is with abuses," Hughes said, "the world is indebted for all the triumphs which have been gained by reason and humanity over error and oppression."

The issue of a free press came before the Supreme Court again in 1964 with an earlier *New York Times* case. This one, *New York Times Co.* v. *Sullivan*, involved an advertisement the *Times* ran on March 29, 1960. The full-page ad sought donations for a committee supporting Dr. Martin Luther King Jr.'s civil rights efforts. Under the heading "Heed Their Rising Voices," the ad related an incident in which Montgomery police were said to have mistreated protesting students. As it turned out, several of the details mentioned in the ad were wrong. In addition, some people were falsely listed as sponsoring the ad.

L. B. Sullivan, the Montgomery police commissioner, complained that the ad defamed him. Although the ad did not mention him by name, Sullivan claimed that the public would associate him with the law-enforcement activities mentioned in the Montgomery story. He sued the *Times* for libel.

The case eventually made its way to the U.S. Supreme Court. In a unanimous decision, the Court ruled against Sullivan. The opinion, written by Justice William J. Brennan Jr., upheld the right of the press to publish criticisms of a public official, even though some of the facts were false. Furthermore, the Court ruled that officials could not sue for libel—even when statements against them were untrue—unless they could prove that the statements were made with "actual malice."

In writing the decision, Brennan noted that "debate on public issues should be uninhibited, robust, and wide-open." Such debates, he added, "may well include vehement, caustic, and sometimes unpleasantly sharp attacks on government and public officials."

Like Justice Hughes, Brennan took particular aim at the Sedition Act of 1798. He noted that in 1840 Congress voted to repay all fines assessed against violators of the act because the law was considered to be unconstitutional. President Jefferson, for the same reason, pardoned anyone who had been convicted under the act's provisions. These actions, Brennan said, reflected a "broad consensus" that the Sedition Act violated the provisions of the First Amendment because it prohibited criticism of the government and officials.

four
THE NEW YORK TIMES GOES TO PRESS

FOR *THE NEW YORK TIMES*, the decision to publish top secret government documents was a complex one that put the publishing company at grave legal and financial risk.

The *Times* consulted Louis M. Loeb, a partner in the prestigious New York law firm of Lord, Day & Lord, on the legality of publishing the secret documents. Seven years earlier, Loeb had been one of the *Times*'s lawyers on the *Sullivan* case, a landmark Supreme Court case that broadened freedom of the press in libel suits. This time, however, Loeb strongly advised against publishing. The lawyer warned that the *Times* would endanger national security and could be charged under the nation's espionage law. *Times* officials could go to jail, he said.

But James Goodale, the in-house lawyer for the *Times*, argued that the First Amendment protected the paper's right to publish. The espionage law, he said, applied to spies, not newspapers. "I said 'Look, I just don't think this statute applies [to the press] . . . and if it does, I don't think it's constitutional. It can't be,'" Goodale recounted in a 1999 interview.

The sixty-two-year-old Loeb, however, violently disagreed. According to Goodale, Loeb said he would not defend the *Times* if it published the papers and was taken to court by the government. Goodale, then thirty-seven, stood his ground.

Times officials also wrestled with the question of whether to print the actual documents contained in the

Pentagon Papers. Ellsberg had believed that publishing the documents themselves was essential. The reporters involved in the project agreed with this opinion. They argued that the documents proved that the information reported in the articles was true. Without the documents, they said, the American people might not believe the *Times* version.

Prominent *Times* columnists James Reston and Tom Wicker, managing editor A. M. Rosenthal, Washington bureau chief Max Frankel, and foreign affairs editor James Greenfield held Goodale's view that the *Times* should publish the series. Harding F. Bancroft, executive vice president of the *Times*, sided with Loeb.

Days of heated argument followed. Finally, publisher Arthur Ochs Sulzberger took Goodale's advice and gave the go-ahead to print the articles and the documents. The editors decided, however, not to refer to the documents as "secret" and to keep the reporting "as low-key as possible." Almost three months after Neil Sheehan had first obtained the study, after weeks of combing through the documents and refining the lead article, the *Times* would break the story of the Pentagon Papers.

presses ROLL

On Sunday, June 13, 1971, Sheehan's story on the Pentagon Papers, next to a picture of Tricia Nixon in her wedding dress, led the day's news. The rather ho-hum headline—"VIETNAM ARCHIVE: PENTAGON STUDY TRACES 3 DECADES OF GROWING U.S. INVOLVEMENT"—downplayed the importance of the *Times*'s decision to publish the top secret report. But some of the findings revealed in the Pentagon study—and in Sheehan's article—were shocking:

- The United States became "directly involved" in Vietnam as a result of President Harry S. Truman's decision to give military aid to French forces in that country.

- Under President Dwight D. Eisenhower's administration, the United States played "a direct role" in the breakdown of talks to settle the conflict in Southeast Asia.

- President Kennedy deepened U.S. involvement in Vietnam by moving from a policy of "limited risk" to one of "broad commitment."

- The Johnson administration planned all-out warfare against North Vietnam in the spring of 1964, a year before informing Congress or the public of U.S. intentions. This occurred at the same time Johnson was running as the peace candidate.

- The United States accelerated bombing of Vietnam despite intelligence reports that increased attacks would not work to end the war or defeat the enemy.

Accompanying Sheehan's story were official cables, memos, and position papers. Among the documents was a summary of a 1965 Defense Department study, which outlined the events surrounding the Tonkin Gulf incident.

In a separate story, *Times* reporter Hedrick Smith described the Pentagon study, its beginnings, and what it did and did not cover. The Pentagon study revealed "that at times the highest Administration officials not only kept information about their real intentions from the press and Congress, but also kept secret from the Government bureaucracy the real motives for their written recommendations or actions," Smith reported.

The Pentagon Papers series filled six pages of the Sunday edition of the *Times*.

EXCErPTS From THE PEnTaGOn Papers

Excerpts from *The Pentagon Papers*, Gravel Edition, published 1971 by Beacon Press:

From Volume 2, Chapter 4, "The Overthrow of Ngo Dinh Diem, May–November, 1963," pp. 201–276. (Boston: Beacon Press, 1971):

In the course of these policy debates [on whether to support a weak Diem administration, go along with his overthrow, or use the instability to withdraw from Vietnam], several participants pursued the logical but painful conclusion that if the war could not be won with Diem, and if his removal would lead to political chaos and also jeopardize the war effort, then the war was probably unwinnable. If that were the case, the argument went, then the U.S. should really be facing a more basic decision on either an orderly disengagement from an irretrievable situation, or a major escalation of the U.S. involvement, including the use of U.S. combat troops. These prophetic minority voices were, however, raising an unpleasant prospect that the Administration was unprepared to face at that time. In hindsight, however, it is clear that this was one of the times in the history of our Vietnam involvement when we were making fundamental choices. The option to disengage honorably at that time now appears an attractively low-cost one. But for the Kennedy Administration then, the costs no doubt appeared much higher. In any event, it proved to be unwilling to accept the implications of predictions for a bleak future. The Administration hewed to the belief that if the U.S. be but willing to exercise its power, it could ultimately always have its way in world affairs.

From Volume 3, Chapter 3, "The Air War in North Vietnam: Rolling Thunder Begins, February–June, 1965," pp. 269–388:

In the closing days of February and during early March, the [Johnson] Administration undertook publicly and privately to defend and propound its rationale for the air strikes, stressing its determination to stand by the GVN [Government of Vietnam, or South Vietnam], but reaffirming the limited nature of its objectives toward North Vietnam. Secretary Rusk conducted a marathon public information campaign to signal a seemingly reasonable but in fact quite tough US position on negotiations, demanding that Hanoi "stop doing what it is doing against its neighbors" before any negotiations could prove fruitful. Rusk's disinterest in negotiations at this time was in concert with the view of virtually all the President's key advisors, that the path to peace was not then open. Hanoi held sway over more than half of South Vietnam and could see the Saigon Government crumbling before her very eyes. The balance of power at this time simply did not furnish the U.S. with a basis for bargaining and Hanoi had no reason to accede to the hard terms the U.S. had in mind. Until military pressures on North Vietnam could tilt the balance of forces the other way, talk of negotiation could be little more than a hollow exercise.

From Volume 4, Chapter 1, "The Air War in North Vietnam, 1965–1968," pp. 1–276:

Under-Secretary of State George Ball sent to his colleagues among the small group of Vietnam "principals" in Washington a memorandum warning that the United States was poised on the brink of a military and political disaster. Neither through expanded bombing of the North nor through a substantial increase in U.S. forces in the South would the United States be likely to achieve its objectives, Ball argued. Instead of escalation, he urged, "we should undertake either to extricate ourselves or to reduce our defense perimeters in South Viet-Nam to accord with the capabilities of a limited US deployment." *"This is our last clear chance to make this decision,"* the Under-Secretary asserted. And in a separate memorandum to the President, he explained why:

The decision you face now, therefore, is crucial. Once large numbers of US troops are committed to direct combat they will begin to take heavy casualties in a war they are ill-equipped to fight in a non-cooperative if not downright hostile countryside.

Once we suffer large casualties we will have started a well-nigh irreversible process. Our involvement will be so great that we cannot—without national humiliation—stop short of achieving our complete objectives. *Of the two possibilities I think humiliation would be more likely than the achievement of our objectives—even after we have paid terrible costs.*

WHITe HOUSe ReaCTION

At the White House, the articles caused little more than a ripple at first. When General Alexander Haig, assistant to Henry Kissinger, called shortly after noon that Sunday, the president quizzed him about casualties in Vietnam. As the discussion wound down, Nixon asked casually, "Nothing else of interest in the world today?" Haig's response was an immediate and angry outburst over the publication of the Pentagon study. "This is a devastating . . . security breach of the greatest magnitude of anything I've ever seen," he told Nixon. The president, on the other hand, seemed much less concerned. He told Haig he hadn't even read the story.

Haig believed the study put former presidents Kennedy and Johnson in a poor light. "It's a tough attack on Kennedy," Haig said, adding, "It's brutal on President Johnson."

The fact that the study would damage Democratic leaders certainly didn't upset the Republican president.

In a follow-up call to Secretary of State William Rogers an hour later, Nixon chatted about the wedding of his daughter, Tricia, the day before. After discussing U.S. casualties in Vietnam, Nixon said he thought the *Times* story wasn't getting much attention nationally. "It's more of a Washington-New York story," he told Rogers. Neither man seemed overly concerned about the *Times* reports. They agreed to talk more about the story and its fallout the following day.

Later that afternoon, Nixon spoke about the *Times* report with Kissinger, who was in California at the time. Kissinger, who had read the study, believed the *Times* piece might even help Nixon in the polls. "This is a gold mine of showing how the previous administration got us in there [Vietnam]," Kissinger told Nixon. "It pins it all on Kennedy and Johnson."

Kissinger did acknowledge, however, that the *Times* report might "hurt a little" regarding the U.S. negotiations then going on with North Vietnam. The report might be interpreted by Hanoi as a "weakening of resolve," Kissinger said.

Nixon surmised that the *Times* had printed the series

to try to influence the debate on the war Congress had scheduled later that week. The debate's focus was the McGovern-Hatfield amendment, a proposal that would cut off all funding for the war by year's end.

Although they initially believed that the *Times* article would not hurt Nixon, both men denounced the person who leaked the study. "It's unconscionable," Nixon said, and Kissinger agreed. "I'm absolutely certain that this violates all sorts of security laws," the national security adviser said. Both men focused their anger on the fact that "whole file cabinets" of secret documents had been leaked to the press. The president declared, "People have gotta be put to the torch for this sort of thing."

The two men explored options of dealing with the person who had leaked the material. Nixon suggested asking for a Congressional hearing into the matter. Kissinger agreed, but said they should wait until after the congressional vote on the McGovern-Hatfield amendment. Nixon ultimately decided to confer with Attorney General John Mitchell to see what should be done about the massive leak.

Near the end of the conversation, the president expressed his concern that similar leaks might reveal his administration's activities in Cambodia and Laos. "You can be sure all that's in some file," he said. Kissinger reassured him, however, that administration officials might record Nixon's orders, but "they weren't in on the reason." Nixon agreed, saying, "Let's not worry about that."

SECOND IN A SERIES

The following day, Monday, June 14, *The New York Times* printed its second installment of the Pentagon Papers story. It focused on Johnson's 1965 decision to bomb North Vietnam.

Later that day, Nixon spoke with his top aide, H. R. Haldeman, about the *Times* series. The president suggested they press criminal charges against the newspaper for printing classified information. Nixon felt no push to take action immediately, however, as long as the law allowed him a year or so to pursue the case. "I don't think we can do much now," Nixon told Haldeman, "but if the statute of limitations is a year. . . I know that we can charge them then."

Haldeman noted that the *Times* report put the government and its officials—including the president—in a bad light. "What it says is . . . you can't trust the government; you can't believe what they say; and you can't rely on their judgment; and the implicit infallibility of presidents, which has been an accepted thing in America, is badly hurt by this, because it shows that people do things the president wants to do even though it's wrong, and the president can be wrong."

PRESIDENT NIXON AND HIS TOP AIDE, H. R. HALDEMAN (LEFT) AGREED THAT THE PENTAGON PAPERS PUT THE ADMINISTRATION IN A BAD LIGHT, BUT THEY DIDN'T BELIEVE THEY COULD TAKE DIRECT ACTION AGAINST *THE NEW YORK TIMES* IMMEDIATELY.

Even so, both Nixon and Haldeman agreed that they couldn't immediately retaliate against the newspaper—at least not publicly. "The story is out; there's nothing you can do about it," Nixon said. "By doing anything we would only escalate it more." However, the president was determined to block *Times* reporters' access to the White House "because of their disloyalty to the country." He told Haldeman, "Don't give 'em anything!" Nixon also told Haldeman to get a sympathetic senator to accuse Leslie "Sam" Gelb and the Brookings Institute (a think tank with Democratic leanings) of leaking the classified documents. Gelb, who had directed the work on the Pentagon Papers, was then working at the Brookings Institute. Nixon believed the think tank was at the center of efforts to discredit his administration.

ATTORNEY GENERAL JOHN MITCHELL
URGED PRESIDENT NIXON TO ISSUE A
SUBPOENA TO HALT CONTINUED PUBLI-
CATION OF THE PENTAGON PAPERS.

Haldeman wrote about the *Times* series in his diary for that day: "The key now is for us to keep out of it and let the people that are affected cut each other up on it."

STOP THE PRESSES

A telephone conversation later that evening with adviser John Ehrlichman apparently convinced Nixon that immediate action could and should be taken. According to Ehrlichman, Attorney General John Mitchell wanted to file a subpoena before the *Times* printed the next day's paper. If no action was taken, Mitchell warned, the government would lose its chance to prosecute the newspaper.

At first Nixon wavered. "I wouldn't prosecute the *Times*," he told Ehrlichman. "My view is to prosecute the [people] that gave it to 'em."

Ehrlichman persisted. "I'd kinda like to have a cause of action against [the *Times*] in case we needed it," he told the president.

At that point, Nixon agreed to discuss the matter with Mitchell.

Shortly afterward, the president called Mitchell to ask his advice on the matter. Mitchell suggested a telegram be sent to the *Times* telling the newspaper that it had violated the law by publishing the documents and warning that it should not print any more. "Otherwise we will look a little foolish in not following through on our legal obligations," Mitchell said.

That convinced Nixon, who already considered the *Times* an enemy of his administration. He gave Mitchell the approval he had been waiting for.

Kissinger, who had just flown in from California, bolstered the view that action should be taken against the newspaper. He reported that former President Johnson would also back any action against the *Times*. According to Kissinger, Johnson believed the *Times*'s publication of the classified documents was "an attack on the whole integrity of government, that if whole file cabinets can be stolen and then made available to the press, you can't have orderly government anymore."

Mitchell told Nixon that the government had taken similar action against newspapers before. However, the government had never before asked the court to prevent a newspaper from printing articles—prior restraint—based on national security concerns. Before hanging up, the attorney general also said that Walt Rostow, Johnson's national security adviser, had identified Daniel Ellsberg, "a left-winger," as the prime suspect in the leak.

On the evening of June 14, Mitchell sent a telegram to *Times* publisher Sulzberger informing him that the Pentagon Papers were classified as top secret and that publication of the material violated the espionage law of the United States. Further publication, the telegram continued, would "cause irreparable injury to the defense interests of the United States." Mitchell directed Sulzberger not to publish any more material from the Pentagon study and to return all top secret materials to the Defense Department.

At about 7:30 p.m., Mitchell's assistant, Robert Mardian, telephoned the *Times* and read the telegram to Bancroft, executive vice president of the *Times*. The printing deadline for Tuesday's first edition was about two hours away.

The *Times* "Respectfully Declines"

Times officials responded with a statement saying the newspaper "must respectfully decline" Mitchell's request. "It is in the interest of the people of this country," the statement continued, "to be informed of the material contained in this series of articles." The issue, the *Times* concluded, was "properly a matter for the courts to decide." The *Times* pledged to obey "the final decision of the court" on the matter.

The following day, June 15, the *Times* published the third installment of its series on the Pentagon study. It detailed Johnson's secret decision to send more troops to South Vietnam in 1965.

Mitchell immediately filed suit in U.S. District Court in New York to stop the *Times* from publishing any further documents from the Pentagon study. The *Times* had so far published three reports on the study. In addition, the newspaper had reproduced several government documents to back the accuracy of the reports.

The lawsuit meant the *Times* would have to appear in court to defend its right to publish. That afternoon, Judge Murray Gurfein heard arguments from the *Times* and the U.S. government. It was the judge's first case since being appointed to the district court bench by Nixon. Mitchell and the president were delighted that Gurfein would hear the case. Before nightfall, Gurfein issued a temporary injunction against the *Times*. He ordered the newspaper to stop publication of the study until a full hearing could be held, which the judge scheduled to take place in three days.

"No such censorship had ever been deemed legal under the First Amendment," the *Times*'s Frankel wrote years later. "But this case inspired frenzied, ominous charges." Frankel recounted how government officials charged that the paper was "violating the Espionage Act—in wartime. Compromising intelligence sources. Inducing, receiving and rewarding the theft of Government property. Delaying, perhaps derailing, efforts to end the war."

NIXON SENDS SIGNAL

On the political front, Nixon and his aides spent the next few days developing a case against the *Times* in the public arena. In a press conference on Tuesday, June 15, Secretary of State Rogers reported that the case had raised foreign governments' concern over the security of their communications to the U.S. government. He added that, unlike previous administrations, the Nixon administration was telling the truth to the American people.

That same day, Nixon and Charles Colson, special counsel to the president, made plans to stir up critics of *The New York Times*. Nixon suggested having veterans' groups, labor leaders, and members of Congress speak against the paper's actions. Colson reported his efforts to generate editorials in other newspapers critical of the *Times*. "The main thing is," Nixon said, "to cast it in terms of doing something disloyal to the country."

In his 1978 memoirs, Nixon said he pushed for the injunction against the *Times* because it was "the role of the government, not *The New York Times*, to judge the impact of a top secret document." If he had taken no action, Nixon said, "it would be a signal to every disgruntled bureaucrat in the government that he could leak anything he pleased while the government simply stood by." Nixon believed that it was the *Times*'s opposition to the war in Vietnam "rather than a consistent attachment to principle" that drove the newspaper to publish the documents.

IN DISTRICT COURT

The court order prevented the *Times* from publishing the Pentagon Papers series on Wednesday, Thursday, and Friday. During that time, Goodale worked to assemble a legal team to represent the newspaper. Loeb and his firm had declined to represent the *Times* in the case. Goodale turned instead to Alexander Bickel, an expert in constitutional law. Bickel, a Yale Law School professor, would serve as lead

JUDGE MURRAY GURFEIN ARRIVES IN THE COURTROOM ON JUNE 19, 1971, TO
DELIVER HIS RULING ON THE PENTAGON PAPERS CASE.

counsel for the *Times*. Although well-versed in law and the media, Bickel had never presented a case in court.

On Friday, June 18, at 10 a.m., Judge Gurfein opened the hearing on the Pentagon Papers case. The government, represented by Whitney North Seymour Jr. and Michael Hess, demanded that the court stop the presses. Seymour was U.S. Attorney for New York, and Hess worked in the civil division of the U.S. Attorney's office. Publication of the documents, the government's lawyers argued, jeopardized the U.S. position in Vietnam and put American soldiers at risk. Continued publication, the lawyers claimed, would cause "irreparable harm to vital national security interests." Four witnesses testified for the government. Part of the proceedings took place in open court. At the request of the government lawyers, some testimony was heard behind closed doors (*in camera*) because it concerned top secret reports.

NOT ENOUGH EVIDENCE

On Friday, June 18, the day of the hearing, the *Washington Post* published documents and articles based on a copy of the Pentagon study that the newspaper had obtained two days earlier. Other newspapers and wire services published reports based on the *Times* and *Post* articles. The *Times*'s lawyers used the publication of the Pentagon Papers in other newspapers in their pleadings before the court. Since other papers were already publishing the information, the *Times*'s lawyers said, it served no purpose to prevent the *Times* from publishing it as well.

Sixteen people submitted affidavits on behalf of the *Times*. Several noted cases in which the government had unnecessarily classified documents as secret. When the documents in these cases were leaked to the press, it became clear that officials wanted to keep them secret for political reasons. In such cases, the *Times* argued, it was the responsibility of the press to inform the public.

The New York hearing ended at 10:30 p.m. after a long, contentious day. On Saturday, June 19, Judge Gurfein rejected the government's request. In a sixteen-page opinion, the judge said that Congress, in passing the espionage laws, had not given the executive branch the authority to stop the presses. However, the judge said, he believed that under the Constitution the president could seek a court injunction against a newspaper when the material about to be published was "absolutely vital to current national security."

In the *Times* case, Gurfein ruled, the government had not presented enough evidence to show that release of the Pentagon Papers would "seriously breach" the nation's security. "No cogent reasons were advanced" to prove the documents would do anything more than embarrass the government, the judge said.

The *Times*, he said, had published the articles "in good faith" and had no intention of causing "injury to the United States."

In a strongly worded passage, Gurfein detailed the importance of freedom of the press:

> The security of the Nation is not at the ramparts alone.
> Security also lies in the value of our free institutions. A

cantankerous press, an obstinate press, a ubiquitous press, must be suffered by those in authority in order to preserve the even greater values of freedom of expression and the right of the people to know. These are troubled times. There is no greater safety valve for discontent and cynicism about the affairs of government than freedom of expression in any form.

Government Appeals

In light of Gurfein's ruling, government attorney Seymour immediately appealed to the U.S. Circuit Court of Appeals for the Second Circuit in New York. The government asked for and got an extension of the injunction barring further publication of the controversial study in the *Times*. A hearing was set for Monday, June 21, before a three-judge panel. Because of the importance of the case, the judges decided to have the full eight-member court hear arguments on June 22.

Before the hearing, Seymour filed a special appendix with the court to strengthen his case. The appendix listed

Arthur Ochs Sulzberger, publisher of *The New York Times*, answers questions about the Pentagon Papers controversy at a press conference at John F. Kennedy Airport.

seventeen items found in the Pentagon Papers that the government claimed would jeopardize national security if published. The first ten items, if made public, threatened ongoing military operations and put U.S. forces in danger, according to the government. Publication of an additional seven items, the government claimed, would delay the Nixon administration's plan to withdraw U.S. troops gradually and leave the fighting in the hands of South Vietnamese soldiers. The appendix was sealed and kept from public view.

In making his arguments to the court, Seymour emphasized three points. First, he said the Pentagon Papers had been properly classified as top secret. Second, Seymour argued that Judge Gurfein should have read the entire Pentagon study before making a ruling on it. Third, the evidence Seymour had submitted showed that if the *Times* continued to publish the study, U.S. military and diplomatic interests would be harmed.

Seymour told the court the government was willing to set up a task force to review the Pentagon study. It would then release as much of the study as possible to the public. He suggested the review could be completed within forty-five days.

In closing, Seymour asked the court to take one of three actions: bar the *Times* from publishing any more of the study, stop the presses until the task force had finished its review, or order Judge Gurfein to hold a new hearing on the case.

Bickel and William E. Hegarty presented the *Times's* case to the court. They argued that the federal government did not have the authority to seek or to get a restraining order to stop the presses in this case. In addition, they said, the government's evidence did not support the claim that the study contained material that would create serious security problems if printed.

In a 5 to 3 decision issued June 23, the court ordered the case back to district court for another review. The ruling

(LEFT TO RIGHT) REPORTER NEIL SHEEHAN, MANAGING EDITOR A. M. ROSENTHAL, AND FOREIGN NEWS EDITOR JAMES L. GREENFIELD IN THE OFFICES OF *THE NEW YORK TIMES* AFTER IT WAS ANNOUNCED THAT THE NEWS-PAPER HAD WON THE PULITZER PRIZE FOR PUBLIC SERVICE FOR PUBLISHING THE PENTAGON PAPERS.

instructed Judge Gurfein to go over the items presented by Seymour and decide which, if any, would pose "grave and immediate danger to the security of the United States" if they were made public. After the review, the *Times* would be banned from printing only those items that Gurfein selected. The court gave Gurfein until July 3 to issue a ruling.

In a terse dissent, the three opposing judges stated that the injunction should be thrown out and the *Times* be allowed to publish.

Times officials had no wish to wait until July 3 for yet another ruling from the lower court. They would take their case to the highest court in the land, the U.S. Supreme Court.

Five
The *Washington Post:*
Keeping Up the Momentum

On Friday, June 18, the *Washington Post* published its own story on the Pentagon Papers. Angered by Judge Gurfein's initial order to the *Times* to stop publishing them, Daniel Ellsberg had given his remaining copies of the Pentagon Papers to reporters from the *Washington Post* and other newspapers. *Washington Post* publisher Katharine Graham described in her memoir how *Post* editor Ben Bagdikian flew to Boston to get the papers from Ellsberg on Wednesday, June 16. The massive document would not fit in Bagdikian's suitcase, and he had to put it in a big box, which he carried with him onto the plane back to Washington. The box, according to Graham, had its own first-class seat next to Bagdikian.

The *Post* endured the same kind of agonized indecision over publishing the top secret documents as had the *Times.* During a lengthy June 17 debate on the newspaper's dilemma, *Post* executive editor Ben Bradlee, editors, and reporters pushed hard for immediate publication.

Graham reported that Bradlee threatened to quit if the *Post* didn't publish the Pentagon Papers. He had worked hard to transform the *Post* into one of the nation's top papers. Not publishing would destroy the newspaper's reputation, Bradlee argued. Furthermore, he said, the paper had to publish the Pentagon Papers story on Friday (the next day) to "keep up the momentum" and send the message that the *Post* would not give in to government pressure against the press.

"CALCULATED MISLEADING OF THE PUBLIC"

The morning of June 17 the *Post* published an editorial applauding the *Times*'s series on the Pentagon Papers. The value of the series, the editorial noted, was that it presented "irrefutable documentation" of successive administrations' "calculated misleading of the public, the purposeful manipulation of public opinion, [and] the stunning discrepancies between public pronouncements and private plans."

The newspaper's attorneys and the chair of its board, however, feared that the *Post* could be prosecuted under the Espionage Act if it published the top secret papers. They also were concerned that legal action could shut down the company's TV stations and threaten the *Post*'s recent stock offerings. In the end, Graham sided with Bradlee and gave her approval just before Friday's deadline.

The *Post* had another problem the *Times* did not face: It had to prepare the Pentagon Papers and write accompanying articles in less than a day. Chalmers Roberts, an experienced *Post* reporter, worked feverishly on the story all day. Meanwhile, a team of researchers and reporters sorted through the documents and fed Roberts the information he needed for his article. Roberts focused on a story not yet covered by *The New York Times*, the Eisenhower administration's interference in Vietnam's 1954 elections. Unlike the *Times*, the *Post* chose not to publish the actual documents.

Roberts's story ran in Friday's second edition. After the lengthy debate on whether to publish, there had not been time to print it in the first edition. The headline blared across the front page: "DOCUMENTS REVEAL U.S. EFFORT IN '54 TO DELAY VIET ELECTION."

GOVERNMENT FILES SUIT

At 3 p.m. Friday, William Rehnquist, then an assistant attorney general, called Bradlee and gave him the same warning the *Times* had received. Bradlee, like the *Times* editors, "respectfully" declined to comply with the government's request not to publish the Pentagon Papers. The government immediately filed suit against the newspaper in U.S. District Court in Washington, D.C.

Ellsberg had also given the papers to several television stations, all of which had decided not to use them in on-air broadcasts. They feared that the Nixon administration would take away their broadcast licenses, which were issued by the Federal Communications Commission, a federal regulatory agency.

Many other newspapers risked prosecution by publishing stories based on the Pentagon Papers. The Associated Press, United Press International, and the *Washington Post-Los Angeles Times* news services funneled the story to hundreds of newspapers around the country. The government sought an injunction against the *Boston Globe* after that newspaper published documents from the Pentagon Papers on June 22. As the court issued orders to one paper to stop publishing, another paper took up the gauntlet and printed its own version of the story. Judge Roger Robb, hearing the case against the *Post* in the circuit court in Washington, D.C., described the courts' efforts to silence the press as riding "herd on a swarm of bees."

WASHINGTON POST IN COURT

While Gurfein heard the *Times* case, Judge Gerhard Gesell reviewed the government's complaint against the *Post* in U.S. District Court in Washington, D.C. At 8:05 p.m. on Friday, June 18, Gesell turned down the government's request for a temporary injunction. The government, the judge ruled, had not proved that publication of the Pentagon Papers would injure the nation. Without such proof, Gesell said, he could not grant "a prior restraint on publication of essentially historical data."

The judge said the government's only recourse was to bring criminal charges against the *Post* after it published the information.

United States district judge Gerhard A. Gesell walks from his home to the court before making a decision about whether to stop publication of the Pentagon Papers. He ruled that publication could proceed.

Late that night the U.S. Circuit Court of Appeals called an emergency session to hear the government's appeal of Gesell's ruling. Appearing before the three-judge panel, the government's lawyer, Kevin T. Maroney, argued that further publication by the *Post* would "irreparably damage national security." He asked the court at the very least to bar the *Post* from publishing until a full court hearing could be held. Roger Clark, representing the *Post*, countered that Judge Gesell's ruling should be upheld.

At 1:20 a.m. on Saturday, in a 2 to 1 decision, the appeals panel overturned Gesell's ruling. It ordered the *Post* to cease publication until a full hearing could be held on the matter in district court. The judges set the hearing for Monday, June 21. The decision came so late, however, that the court allowed the *Post* to distribute that day's newspapers, which carried more reports on the Pentagon Papers.

During the Monday hearing in district court, lawyers for both sides made most of their arguments behind closed doors. *Post* publisher Graham recalled that the windows in the courtroom were blacked out to prevent the public from viewing the proceedings. The government lawyers requested the closed hearing so that they could make their case without disclosing secrets contained in the Pentagon Papers. The *Post* opposed the secret court proceedings, but Judge Gesell overruled their objections.

TOO MANY SECRETS

In defending the *Post*'s right to publish, lead attorney William R. Glendon questioned the legitimacy of the government's classification system. He argued that many government documents were unnecessarily classified as secret. Glendon pointed to several instances where such material had been leaked to the press and published without harm to the nation's security. In these cases, Glendon noted, the press had acted responsibly and had not printed information that threatened the nation. Because the government kept so many documents secret, the *Post* lawyer argued, the press was forced to use classified material in order to keep the American public informed about what its leaders were doing.

In addition, Glendon said, much of the material in the Pentagon Papers had already been published or was widely known.

Government lawyer Maroney followed much the same arguments made three days earlier in the *Times* case. He claimed that publishing the Pentagon study would damage U.S. diplomatic relations with countries named in the documents, interfere with ongoing negotiations, and reveal war plans that the United States might still use.

Unswayed, District Court Judge Gesell again ruled in favor of the *Post*. Gesell acknowledged that publishing the Pentagon Papers might interfere with "delicate negotiations" and embarrass those involved in diplomacy. Nevertheless, he said, the government had not proved that publication would cause a "definite break in diplomatic relations" or lead to "an armed attack on the United States" or its allies, result in a war, or hurt military plans, intelligence operations, or scientific and technological systems.

The First Amendment, Gesell ruled, did not permit "a prior restraint on publication" in this case because the government failed to show "an immediate grave threat to the national security."

APPEALS COURT UPHOLDS RULING

Shortly after Judge Gesell issued his decision, the U.S. Circuit Court of Appeals for the District of Columbia agreed to hear the government's appeal. The hearing was scheduled for the next day, Tuesday, June 22, at 2 p.m. The court also continued to ban the *Post* from publishing the Pentagon Papers.

Tuesday's hearing introduced a new player to the case. At the request of Attorney General John Mitchell, U.S. Solicitor General Erwin N. Griswold argued the government's case before the court. Griswold had been dean of Harvard Law School for decades before becoming President Johnson's solicitor general. He had continued in that post under the Nixon administration. Despite his prestige, however, Griswold failed to convince the appeals court to overturn Judge Gesell's ruling.

As in the *Times* case, the *Post* hearing was overseen by the full court. The government based its arguments on the claim that the Pentagon Papers were correctly classified as top secret, that the president had "sole discretion" to manage foreign affairs, and that the court had no business second-guessing him. Affidavits from government witnesses contained much of the same material in the special appendix filed in New York.

Lawyers for the *Post* focused on First Amendment guarantees of a free press. The government, they argued, could stop the presses only if it could prove, in Gesell's words, an "immediate grave threat" to the nation would be caused by publishing.

On Wednesday, June 23, seven of the nine judges voted to uphold Gesell's decision in favor of the *Post*. The ruling specifically mentioned the *Near v. Minnesota* decision, noting that the government had failed to meet the standard set in that case. "The government's proof," the opinion read, "does not justify an injunction."

The two dissenting judges would have allowed the government a second hearing to prove its case. In his dissent, Judge Malcolm R. Wilkey concluded that at least some of the material in the government documents "could clearly result in great harm to the nation." He described "harm" as "the death of soldiers, the destruction of alliances, the greatly increased difficulty of negotiation with our enemies, [and] the inability of our diplomats to negotiate."

The appeals court also denied a government appeal filed on June 24 to send the case back to district court as the New York court had. In denying the request, the court stated that the government "had had an adequate opportunity to establish its case."

As before, the court extended the ban on publishing until an appeal could be heard. This time the government would take its appeal to the Supreme Court.

POLITICAL RESPONSE

Like the White House, the American public reacted slowly to the *Times*'s series on the Pentagon Papers. Few readers waded through the six full pages of newsprint devoted to the series. Other news media paid little attention to the Pentagon study that Sunday.

The following night, however, Howard K. Smith at ABC News and NBC's David Brinkley led off with the story. Walter Cronkite of CBS News devoted almost one-quarter of the on-air broadcast to the matter, as did NBC. In his report on the issue on June 15, NBC's Brinkley noted that classifying documents as top secret had sometimes been done "for political reasons as well as security reasons."

Two days later, all three networks reported that Daniel Ellsberg had been identified as the source of the leak. In a commentary on the situation, ABC's Harry Reasoner attacked government officials' "deception of the American people" and their "intense hypocrisy." He ended that night's broadcast with the statement: "Democracy requires morality."

Members of Congress, some of whom had already seen the study, responded in a variety of ways. Opponents of the war applauded the *Times* series. Those who supported the government's handling of the war were angry that the newspaper had leaked government secrets. Members on both sides of the issue, however, were furious over being deceived by past administrations.

Senator Charles Mathias, R-Maryland, fumed, "I am outraged—but I'm worn down with outrage." The disdain presidents showed for Congress—revealed in the Pentagon Papers—was nothing new, Senator George Aiken, R-Vermont, said. "For a long time, the Executive Branch has tended to regard Congress as a foreign enemy—to be told as little as possible," he declared.

Senate Majority Leader Michael "Mike" Mansfield, D-Montana, said he was "delighted" the study had been made public. Antiwar Senator Frank Church, D-Idaho, said he found nothing in the report that damaged national security and called the court's restraining order censorship.

Senate Minority Leader Hugh Scott, R-Pennsylvania, on the other hand, charged that the documents had been stolen. Senator W. Stuart Symington, D-Missouri, asked the administration to provide copies of the study to the Senate Foreign Relations Committee. Secretary of Defense Melvin R. Laird denied the request, noting pointedly that the papers remained classified.

In the House, Representative Abner J. Mikva, D-Illinois, charged that the court's restraining order against the *Times* "damaged the Bill of Rights." On June 17, sixty-three members of Congress petitioned President Nixon to release the Pentagon Papers. On June 28, the Nixon administration delivered the documents to Congress.

Senator Fulbright, who had previously been given many of the documents by Ellsberg, said he believed the *Times* had "performed a public service" when it published the report.

The Senate was debating the McGovern-Hatfield amendment the week the *Times* published the Pentagon Papers. First introduced by Senators George McGovern and Mark Hatfield the year before as an add-on to the appropriations bill, the amendment aimed to cut off funds for military actions in Cambodia within thirty days and in Laos and Vietnam by the end of 1971. It had failed by a 55 to 39 vote in 1970.

On June 15, two senators—Herman E. Talmadge, D-Georgia, and B. Everett Jordan, D-North Carolina—announced they had changed their opinion on the war and were now calling for the United States to withdraw. The U.S. Conference of Mayors was also urging Nixon to end the war by December 31, 1971, or sooner. Neither their position nor the publication of the Pentagon Papers had much effect on the final vote in the Senate, which defeated the amendment by a 55 to 42 vote on June 16. The House defeated a similar measure a day later. Although many similar resolutions were proposed, none passed. On June 22, however, the Senate approved a resolution proposed by Majority Leader Mansfield that made it "national policy" to withdraw from Southeast Asia within nine months, providing American prisoners of war were released. The measure was not binding on the president.

In the wake of the controversy, *Times* publisher Sulzberger denied that the newspaper had breached national security. Echoing Brinkley's earlier statement, he noted that the secret classification "enables the government to keep embarrassing information from the public."

Military officials challenged Sulzberger's claims. They warned that the Pentagon Papers might enable enemies to decipher U.S. codes. General Maxwell Taylor said Americans needed "to know enough to be good citizens" but did not need information that could damage the government. The publication of secret government documents, he said, set "a precedent for officials betraying government secrets" and harmed relations with other countries.

MANHUNT LAUNCHED

While the nation debated the issues brought to light in the Pentagon Papers, the man who had leaked the documents disappeared from view. Shortly after the government took the *Times* to court, Ellsberg and his wife went into hiding. The government launched what the FBI called "the biggest manhunt since the Lindbergh kidnapping." For twelve days, the couple eluded capture. During a clandestine interview with CBS-TV's Cronkite, filmed at an undisclosed Cambridge, Massachusetts, home, Ellsberg said he had enjoyed reading the news reports on the Pentagon Papers. "I've been reading the truth about the war in the public press," he said, "and it's like breathing clean air." The June 23 broadcast devoted almost ten minutes to Ellsberg. He told Cronkite that it "must be painful" for Americans to discover that leaders they respected "regarded them contemptuously."

On June 28, 1971, Ellsberg surrendered to federal agents. Arrested and charged with six counts of espionage, six of theft, and one for conspiracy, Ellsberg, then forty years old, faced up to 115 years in prison for his Pentagon Papers activities. More than 25,000 people donated money to help pay for Ellsberg's defense and that of his friend, Anthony J. Russo Jr., who was charged as a co-conspirator.

SIX
BEFORE THE SUPREME COURT

On June 24, 1971, *The New York Times* asked the Supreme Court to review the Second Circuit Court's decision. The newspaper also asked the Court to end the injunction that had stopped its publication of the Pentagon Papers for the past nine days. That same afternoon, the government filed a petition with the Supreme Court to hear the *Post* case.

The U.S. Supreme Court hears only a small portion of the thousands of cases submitted for review each year. Most of the time, lawyers file a petition with the Court requesting that their case be heard and outlining why the Court should consider it. This is called a petition for certiorari. *Certiorari* means "to be more fully informed." In most cases, the Court denies the petition, and the lower court's decision remains in force. If the Court does grant *certiorari*, the records of the case are transferred from the lower courts to the Supreme Court, so that the justices will be "fully informed" of the proceedings.

Cases are usually first heard in a state or federal court. If those on the losing side are not satisfied with the decision, they can appeal it, taking it to the next higher court for a ruling. Those appealing the case are called the *appellants*. In Supreme Court cases, they are called *petitioners*. Those on the other side are referred to as *appellees*, or *respondents*, at the Supreme Court level. The higher court reviews the case and decides whether or not to hear it.

This procedure is followed all the way up to the U.S. Supreme Court.

As the highest court in the land, the U.S. Supreme Court rules on cases that will set standards of law for the nation. Judges in lower courts use Supreme Court decisions as guides when issuing their own rulings. To be accepted for review by the Supreme Court, cases must deal with one of three issues: constitutional rights or questions, a conflict between rulings of different courts, or a ruling by a state court on a federal law.

Usually the chief justice selects cases he believes are important and submits the list to the other justices during a private conference. The eight associate justices review the list and discuss their views on whether cases should be scheduled for a hearing. To be heard, a case must get the votes of at least four of the nine justices.

It can take several years for some cases to reach the high Court. In matters of extreme urgency, however, the Court can agree to hear a case without delay.

Because of the importance of questions being raised in the newspaper cases, the Supreme Court justices began discussing the cases that afternoon. Four justices—Chief Justice Warren E. Burger, John Marshall Harlan, Byron R. White, and Harry A. Blackmun—argued to postpone the matter until the fall term. Each Court term runs from October to June or July, depending on the caseload. The justices wanted to block the publication of the controversial Pentagon study until after the Court had ruled on the case. That would mean the newspapers would not be allowed to print the study at least until October, more than three months away.

The four liberal members of the Court—William O. Douglas, Hugo L. Black, William J. Brennan Jr., and Thurgood Marshall—found this totally unacceptable. They believed the injunction should be lifted immediately and the newspapers allowed to print the documents. To delay the presses until fall, they believed, was unthinkable.

CHIEF JUSTICE WARREN E. BURGER PRESIDED OVER THE COURT THAT HEARD
THE PENTAGON PAPERS CASE.

Justice Potter Stewart became the tie-breaker. He
agreed that the press should be restrained from publishing
while the Court considered the case. But he believed the case
was too important to delay for three months. As a compromise, the Court kept the press ban in place but scheduled
oral arguments in two days' time. The lawyers would present
their cases on June 26, at a very rare Saturday session.

Lawyers on both sides would have to file their briefs on the
case before oral arguments. Briefs are the legal documents in
which lawyers outline the facts of their cases and make their
arguments. In them, they cite laws that support their case and
answer charges made by lawyers for the other side. The justices
study the briefs, using the arguments to help them decide the case.

In most instances, lawyers take months to prepare the
complex written arguments to prove their case. The lawyers in
the Pentagon Papers cases, however, would have little more
than twenty-four hours to prepare their briefs.

The government lawyers had an additional burden. The Supreme Court had asked them to provide a complete list of all documents they believed would cause "grave and immediate danger" to the nation if published. In addition to the items listed in the special appendix, the government added a list of eleven items. The additional list was so broad, the newspapers charged, that it covered practically all the newsworthy material in the Pentagon study.

THE BRIEFS

Supreme Court justices rely on previous rulings for guidance in making their decisions. They are much more likely to follow the reasoning already established in a past ruling than to overturn a previous Court decision. There are times, however, when the justices encounter a case in which no previous opinion applies. In rare cases, the justices may overrule an opinion they believe was wrong.

In their briefs, both the *Post* and the *Times* relied on several suits decided previously by the Court to prove their point.

The sixty-one-page brief filed by Alexander Bickel, William E. Hegarty, Lawrence McKay, and James Goodale for the *Times* used several arguments to bolster its case. The first argument focused on the First Amendment, which, in the words of the Court itself, recognized that "a free press is a condition of a free society."

The First Amendment, the brief noted, "peculiarly disfavored" prior restraints on publication. "Prior restraints fall on speech with a brutality and a finality. . . ." The brief went on to say that prior restraints were much more effective in limiting free speech than were criminal penalties imposed after something had been published. "A prior restraint . . . stops more speech, more effectively. A criminal statute chills. The prior restraint freezes."

The brief accepted the premise, noted in the *Near* case, that prior restraints of the press might be allowed in rare cases—but only if publication led "directly and almost unavoidably to a disastrous event for the country." It was "inconceivable" that the government could meet that condition in this case, according to the brief.

Further, the *Times*'s lawyers argued in the brief that the president lacked the authority to order prior restraint. There was no national emergency or other circumstance under which he could claim such power.

In addition, the brief argued, under the separation of powers as set up in the Constitution, the president did not have the power to stop the presses without an act of Congress. And Congress had never passed a law granting government (or the president) the power to seek a prior restraint against the press. Many defenders of the First Amendment, including justices on the Supreme Court, attacked this segment of the argument. They contended that Congress had no authority to put restraints on the First Amendment, which specifically stated, in part, that "Congress shall make no law . . . abridging the freedom of speech, or of the press." Nevertheless, Bickel clung to the argument, believing it bolstered his view that the president, without support from Congress, could not restrain publication.

Finally, the brief said, the government's witnesses had failed to show that publication of the Pentagon Papers would pose a "grave and immediate danger" to America's security. They had not established any direct, specific, and immediate link between the *Times*'s publication of the papers and irreparable injury to the United States. Therefore, the brief concluded, the government's case should be dismissed.

The *Times*'s lawyers argued that either the case should be resolved quickly or the injunction should be lifted. Otherwise, they contended, the Court would be imposing a prior restraint that did not meet the strict standards required by the Constitution.

Likewise, the *Post*'s twenty-six-page brief contended that the government had not proved "an immediate and grave threat to the national security." It, too, cited the strict standards set in the *Near* case, which, it claimed, the government

THrouGH THe courT sYsTem

First Stop: State Court

Almost all cases (about 95 percent) start in state courts. These courts go by various names depending on the state in which they operate: circuit, district, municipal, county, or superior courts. The case is tried and decided by a judge, a panel of judges, or a jury.

The side that loses can then appeal to the next level.

First Stop: Federal Court

U.S. DISTRICT COURT—About 5 percent of cases begin their journey in federal court. Most of these cases concern federal laws, the U.S. Constitution, or disputes that involve two or more states. They are heard in one of the ninety-four U.S. District Courts in the nation.

U.S. COURT OF INTERNATIONAL TRADE—Federal court cases involving international trade appear in the U.S. Court of International Trade.

U.S. CLAIMS COURT—The U.S. Claims Court hears federal cases that involve more than $10,000, Indian claims, and some disputes with government contractors

The loser in federal court can appeal to the next level.

Appeals: State Cases

Forty states have appeals courts that hear cases that have come from the state courts. In states without an appeals court, the case goes directly to the state supreme court.

Appeals: Federal Cases

U.S. CIRCUIT COURT—Cases appealed from U.S. District Courts go to U.S. Circuit courts of appeals. There are twelve circuit courts that handle cases from throughout the nation. Each district court and every state and territory are assigned to one of the twelve circuits. Appeals in few state cases—those that deal with rights guaranteed by the U.S. Constitution—are also heard in this court.

U.S. COURT OF APPEALS—Cases appealed from the U.S. Court of International Trade and the U.S. Claims Court are heard by the U.S. Court of Appeals for the Federal Circuit.

Further Appeals: State Supreme Court
Cases appealed from state appeals courts go to the highest court in the state—usually called the supreme court. In New York, the state's highest court is called the court of appeals. Most state cases do not go beyond this point.

Final Appeals: U.S. Supreme Court
The Supreme Court is the highest court in the country. Its decision on a case is the final word. The Court decides issues that can affect every person in the nation.

The Court selects the cases it will hear—usually around one hundred each year. Four of the nine justices must vote to consider a case in order for it to be heard. Almost all cases have been appealed from the lower courts (either state or federal).

Most people seeking a decision from the Court submit a petition for certiorari. These petitions ask that the case be moved from a lower court to a higher court for review. The Court receives about seven thousand of these requests annually. The petition outlines the case and gives reasons why the Court should review it.

In rare cases, for example *New York Times* v. *United States*, an issue must be decided immediately. When such a case is of national importance, the Court may allow it to bypass the lower court and will hear the case directly.

To win a spot on the Court's docket, a case must fall within one of the following categories:

· Disputes between states and the federal government or between two or more states. The Court also reviews cases involving ambassadors, consuls, and foreign ministers.

· Appeals from a state court that has ruled on a federal question.

· Appeals from federal appeals courts (about two-thirds of all requests fall into this category).

had not met. According to the brief, the justices should not accept the government's top secret label as proof in the case but should examine the record themselves.

Both newspapers noted that the Pentagon Papers had been leaked to other news media. Stopping the presses of the *Times* and the *Post*, they contended, would not keep the study from being made public.

In its brief, the U.S. government also cited the *Near* case in its claim that the Constitution allowed bans on publication when it would cause "grave and immediate danger to the security of the United States." The release of the Pentagon Papers, the brief contended, would result in such danger.

The brief mentioned copyright laws and cease-and-desist orders prohibiting companies from promoting certain illegal trade arrangements as examples of communications barred by the court.

The government also argued that the president's position as commander-in-chief gave him the power to seek an injunction against the press when national security was threatened. The president's control over foreign affairs gave him similar authority, according to the brief.

In addition to the public briefs, both sides submitted sealed briefs available only to the Court. Griswold also filed a motion that at least a portion of the hearing be held behind closed doors as in the lower courts. He wanted to be able to discuss with the Court the classified material the government was trying to keep secret. The Supreme Court accepted the secret briefs but denied the closed hearing.

In many court cases, groups that agree with one side or the other want to offer their views on the issue. Such a group is called *amicus curiae*, meaning "friend of the court." In some cases, the Court allows lawyers for these groups to testify during oral arguments. Usually, though, they are allowed to submit their views only in briefs, which was true in the Pentagon Papers case. The American Civil Liberties Union, the National Emergency Civil Liberties Committee, and a group representing twenty-seven members of Congress submitted briefs supporting the newspapers' right to publish.

The Arguments

On the morning of June 26, 1971, news reporters crowded into the nation's highest court. Inside the courtroom, the lawyers—seated in leather chairs facing the bench—waited for the justices to arrive. The magnificence of the room reflected the momentous decisions that were made there. Twenty-four columns of Italian marble supported the forty-four-foot-high ceiling. Hanging high above the justices' gleaming wooden bench, a large, round clock ticked away the minutes.

Each side has one-half hour to argue the case. On rare occasions, the Court grants a longer time for arguments, but the extension has to be approved in advance. Five minutes before the end of the argument, the court marshal turns on a white light on the lectern. A red light switches on to indicate that time has expired. Occasionally justices will continue to ask questions at the end of an argument. Only then will a lawyer be allowed to talk beyond his or her allotted time.

A lawyer engrossed in his argument might fail to notice the light. If so, he or she might look up to see the nine black-robed justices glaring down. At times, a long-winded lawyer has lifted his head only to see an empty bench, the justices, impatient, having retreated behind the red velvet drapes into their private chambers.

At the clerk's call, everyone rose as the justices entered and sat on the raised platform behind the bench. Chief Justice Burger sat in the center seat. A former assistant attorney general and appeals court judge, Burger joined the Court in 1969 after nomination to the post by President Nixon. To his right and left sat the associate justices.

Black, the longest-serving member, had been on the Court since 1937. Appointed by Franklin D. Roosevelt, Black firmly believed in an absolute freedom of the press, guaranteed by the First Amendment.

Douglas, the second most senior justice, had taught at Columbia and Yale Law Schools and served as chair of the Securities and Exchange Commission before his appointment to the Court in 1939. He, too, had been nominated by Roosevelt. A fierce believer in individual rights over government power, Douglas was known for his independent and generally liberal views.

Harlan, nominated to the Court in 1955 by President Dwight D. Eisenhower, had served as assistant U.S. attorney, had been a special assistant to the attorney general of New York, and had sat on the U.S. Circuit Court of Appeals. He was named for his grandfather, Supreme Court Justice John Marshall Harlan, who served on the Court from 1877 to 1911. The current justice, like his grandfather, was a champion of both state and individual rights.

Before being appointed to the Court by Eisenhower, Stewart had worked briefly as a Wall Street lawyer and had served on the Sixth Circuit Court of Appeals. He joined the Court in 1958.

Brennan, another Eisenhower nominee, joined the Court in 1956. Brennan had served as a New Jersey superior court judge and as an associate judge on that state's supreme court before being named to the high Court.

White, one of only two justices nominated by President Kennedy, had served as deputy U.S. attorney general in Kennedy's administration before his appointment in 1962.

Marshall, the Court's only African-American member, was nominated by President Johnson in 1967. He served as a judge for the Second Circuit Court of Appeals from 1961 to 1965. President Johnson appointed him U.S. solicitor general in 1965. Marshall usually sided with Brennan, Black, and Douglas on the liberal wing of the Court.

Blackmun, the most recent appointee to the Court, was nominated by President Nixon in 1970. He had been a Circuit judge for the Eighth Court of Appeals from 1959 until he joined the Court. Court observers coupled Blackmun and the chief justice, dubbing them the

"Minnesota Twins," because they had been boyhood friends while growing up in Minnesota.

THE GOVERNMENT'S ARGUMENTS

At 11 a.m., the justices signaled they were ready to hear the case. Solicitor General Griswold, representing the government, would begin and end the arguments. As the respondent in the *Times* case and petitioner in the *Post* suit, he would have a total of one hour. Bickel, as attorney for the *Times*, would follow. Glendon would then argue for the *Washington Post*. Griswold would again address the Court to rebut arguments made by the other attorneys.

Thus began a lively discussion. For the next two hours and thirteen minutes, the justices listened to arguments and asked questions about the two cases.

Griswold began by outlining the questions involved in the case: freedom of the press pitted against the "right of the government to function." These two competing principles, he said, must be resolved.

He discarded the view, held by Justice Black among others, that the First Amendment never allowed prior restraint of the press. "I suggest," he told the justices, "that there is no such constitutional rule, and never has been such a constitutional rule."

Bickel and Glendon had acknowledged early on that the First Amendment, in certain circumstances, allowed prior restraint. However, they argued, the government could stop the presses only under the most narrow circumstances. Publication had to cause damage to the national security that was both immediate and grave. The Pentagon Papers, both newspapers claimed, did not meet that condition.

At the heart of the case, Griswold said, was a dispute over whether the government's claimed damages were severe enough to override the press's right to publish. Griswold contended that the eleven items detailed in the special list met that standard. But, he said, even if the Court did not find those particular items of concern, the publication of some material in the overall study would inevitably damage the nation. Government officials simply had not had time, the lawyer argued, to pick out every harmful item in the massive study.

"There are forty-seven volumes of material and millions of words, and there are people in various agencies of the government who have to be consulted," he told the Court. "There simply has not been a full, careful consideration of this material."

Justice Brennan questioned Griswold about the publication of the material by other newspapers. "Am I correct," he asked, "that the injunctions so far granted against the *Times* and the *Post* haven't stopped other newspapers from publishing materials based on this study or kindred papers?" If so, he asked, wouldn't a Court-ordered injunction against the *Times* and the *Post* be a waste of time?

Griswold acknowledged that other papers had published reports on the Pentagon Papers. But, he noted, the articles had been rewrites of those appearing in the *Post* and the *Times* and, as far as he knew, had not revealed new information.

The solicitor general went on to detail the government's plan to review the entire study and release portions of it not vital to national security. The review, he said, would take a minimum of forty-five days. The government would not undertake the review, however, if the Court ruled against prior restraint. "The Court will, in effect, have declassified the materials," Griswold replied.

In response to questions from Justice Stewart, Griswold admitted that much of the government's classified material did not need to be kept secret. He added that the government had been "too slow" in declassifying documents, but noted that the administration was "in the process" of solving the problem. Earlier that year President Nixon had ordered a review of the classification system.

White next asked about criminal prosecution. Griswold

replied that if the government lost the case, it would not be practical to take the newspapers to criminal court over the matter. "I find it exceedingly difficult to think that any jury would convict, or that an appellate court would affirm a conviction of a criminal offense, for the publication of materials which this Court had said could be published."

Under further questioning, Griswold agreed with Stewart that the case revolved around the potential damage that could be caused by the release of the material—regardless of how it was classified.

Justice Harlan, however, disagreed. "I think... the question of classification has an important bearing on the question," he told Griswold. A document classified as top secret, for example, might be more likely to warrant review by the court. Griswold, however, did not pursue this line of argument.

Instead, he contended that Judge Gesell had used too strict a standard in judging whether publication of government documents should be allowed. He asked the Court to set a broader standard. Publication, he said, would cause "irreparable harm" to the nation's security, and that standard—rather than "immediate harm"—should be used. "It [publication] will affect lives," he told the justices. "It will affect the process of the termination of the war. It will affect the process of recovering prisoners of war."

He also argued that publication of negotiations with other countries would impede the president's ability to conduct future negotiations. Even if the published material did not cause immediate problems, Griswold said, foreign governments would be hesitant to enter into secret talks with a nation that could not keep secrets.

Concluding his remarks, Griswold said: "In the whole diplomatic area the things don't happen at 8:15 tomorrow morning. It may be weeks, or months. . . . I think that to say that it can only be enjoined if there will be a war tomorrow morning, when there's a war now going on, is much too narrow."

THE *TIMES* ARGUES

Griswold sat down, and Chief Justice Burger asked Bickel to present the *Times*'s case. Bickel had never argued before the Supreme Court. In fact, he had presented only this one case in the lower courts before facing the highest court in the nation. As a young man, however, he had served as a law clerk to Justice Felix Frankfurter at the time the Court heard the landmark case, *Brown* v. *Board of Education*. In that role, Bickel had often viewed the Court in session and was familiar with its workings.

He began by noting that the *Times* had published three articles by the time the government sought an injunction against the newspaper. "No great alarm sounded" at the White House, he noted, "despite what is now said to be the 'gravest kind of danger.'"

Bickel had spoken only two sentences when Chief Justice Burger interrupted. "Aren't you going to allow some time for somebody to really see what this means, before they act?" he asked the *Times* lawyer.

Without disagreeing, Bickel continued with his argument. The government, he said, had not asked the lower court for more time to prepare its case. And despite Judge Gurfein's repeated requests for more specific examples of how publication would endanger the nation, the government did not produce the required evidence, Bickel said. Lack of time wasn't the problem, he said. "I think the Government gave Judge Gurfein all it had."

Bickel noted that since Congress had never passed a law on prior restraint, the president could invoke a prior restraint only under his own authority. For that to be permitted, Bickel suggested, the president would have to show that publication would result in a "direct, and immediate, and visible" danger to the nation.

That had not happened in this case, according to Bickel. "I am flatly persuaded that there's nothing in there [the list of items submitted by Griswold]. Because if there . . . were, it surely should have turned up by now."

Justice Stewart presented Bickel with a hypothetical case. "Let us assume that . . . we find something [in the sealed record] that absolutely convinces us that its disclosure would result in the sentencing to death of 100 young men whose only offense had been that they were 19 years old, and had low draft numbers. What should we do?"

Bickel replied that he wished Congress had passed a law dealing with such matters so that the nation did not have to rely solely on the president to make such a judgment call.

Stewart pushed for an answer to his question. Finally, Bickel admitted that he would not want such material disclosed—even though the deaths of one hundred soldiers would not necessarily threaten national security. "I'm afraid my inclinations of humanity overcome the somewhat more abstract devotion to the First Amendment, in a case of that sort." But the professor said he was "as confident as I can be of anything" that the Court would not find such a situation in the Pentagon Papers.

Chief Justice Burger then asked Bickel for his views if the disclosure delayed the release of prisoners for a long time. The harm would not be immediate, in that case.

Bickel replied that the link between disclosure and the harm caused would have to be "direct and immediate" in order to prevent publication. If there were other factors involved, Bickel said, then stopping the presses wouldn't be justified. "That is a risk that the First Amendment signifies that this society is willing to take. That is part of the risk of freedom."

He repeated his view that without a law passed by Congress, the president lacked the authority to issue a prior restraint in the Pentagon Papers case. It was a position that surprised and angered those on the Court who believed Congress had no power over the First Amendment.

At that point, Justice Douglas intervened. How, he asked, could Congress pass a law allowing prior restraint when the First Amendment specifically said that "Congress shall make no law abridging freedom of the press"?

Bickel fumbled as he tried to answer the question. He said he had conceded that there could be limits to the First Amendment's guarantee of freedom of the press.

"That's a very strange argument for the *Times* to be making, that the Congress can make all this illegal by passing laws," Justice Douglas countered.

Bickel responded that he "didn't really argue that."

Chief Justice Burger turned the conversation to a new subject. He noted that on one hand, reporters claimed the right not to reveal sources to the government or anyone else. On the other hand, Burger said, the press insisted that the government had no right to keep its information secret.

"Newspaper reporters . . . claim for themselves a right which this argument now would deny to the Government," the chief justice said.

The situation seemed unfair, Bickel acknowledged. But, he noted, reporters didn't shield their sources for themselves, "but rather . . . to vindicate the First Amendment and those interests which that great document serves."

With that, Bickel ended his arguments and sat down.

THE *WASHINGTON POST* RESPONDS

The Court had been in session for almost an hour and a half when Glendon stood to make his case for the *Washington Post*. Glendon turned from Stewart's hypothetical case involving the deaths of one hundred soldiers to the facts of the case at hand. Like Bickel, he argued that the government had not brought to light any specific items that would cause irreparable injury to the nation if published. "What we have heard," he told the Court, "is much more in the nature of conjecture and surmise."

Such conjecture, Glendon said, "that diplomatic negotiations would be made more difficult or embarrassing, does not justify suspending the First Amendment." He repeated Judge Gurfein's statement that people got "the jitters" when there was a security leak. "And I think," Glendon said, "maybe the Government has a case of the jitters here, but that, I submit, does not warrant the stopping of the press on this matter."

He discounted the government's claim that the rush to judgment had prevented a thorough review of the case. The government was given "the fullest hearing," and the lower courts "had plenty of time to consider the matter," he said. On the other hand, Glendon said, the delay in publishing the documents deprived the readers of the *Post* and the *Times* of their right to know.

Glendon next questioned the classification of the Pentagon Papers. The entire study, he noted, had been classified as top secret by "some unknown individual . . . whose judgment couldn't be explored . . . [who] decided that they were 'Top Secret.'" Government officials, he argued, may classify documents as secret in order to prevent the release of embarrassing information. He noted, also, that as a result of the court case, the administration had finally turned the study over to Congress for review.

During the course of the trial, Glendon pointed out, the government had offered to review the study and declassify portions of it. The *Post* lawyer categorized the offer as "some sort of an admission that the original classification . . . was wrong."

Glendon noted that some of the documents dated back to 1945. "The document itself is entitled 'The History'," he told the Court. "From what I've seen of it, that's what it is."

Chief Justice Burger again questioned the fairness of the newspapers' position. The press was determined to protect its sources—by not revealing which documents it possessed—while demanding that it be allowed to reveal the government's secrets, the chief justice noted. Such questions of fairness, he insisted, should be addressed when two parties come into a court hearing. Glendon made the point, to much laughter, that the *Post* did not enter into the suit voluntarily, but was brought in "kicking and screaming."

The lawyer noted that government officials frequently leaked documents to the press and "nothing has happened." Therefore, to claim that the leak of the Pentagon Papers "shocked or appalled" foreign allies, Glendon said, "simply is not so." He added, "This happens. This is one of the facts of life."

In response to a question from the Court, he did acknowledge that it wasn't "customary for the government to leak forty-seven volumes at a time."

Glendon returned to his central argument: that the government had not proved that the publication of any of the Pentagon Papers would cause grave harm to the nation. It was up to the government, not the courts, to produce evidence to back up their claims, he said.

"As I understand it," Glendon told the Court, "when you bring a case you're supposed to prove it; and, when you come in claiming 'irreparable injury,' particularly in this area of the First Amendment, you have a very, very heavy burden."

Black was the last to question Glendon. Like Douglas, he read the First Amendment. The lawyers for both newspapers, Black said, had argued that Congress could make a law to limit the First Amendment's freedom of the press. This was a position Black clearly did not support. Glendon quickly denied that he had said such a thing. "Never. I do not say it. . . . No sir. I say we stand squarely and exclusively on the First Amendment."

Burger thanked him and he sat down.

GRISWOLD'S REBUTTAL

Griswold began his final arguments in the case. The government, he said, was not trying to protect anybody from embarrassing leaks. It was not interested in the past. The government filed suit, he said, to protect the nation from present danger that would be caused by the study's release.

The reason prior restraints had not been used against other leaks, he said, was because the press published the material before the government could take action. The newspapers published the Pentagon Papers as a series. After the first series was printed, the government knew that additional documents would be published.

If a prior restraint was granted, Justice Marshall asked, wouldn't the federal courts become a "censorship board"? Griswold bristled at the suggestion: "That's a pejorative way to put it," he said. "I don't know what the alternative is."

Justice Black had a quick answer: "The First Amendment might be." The comment brought laughter from the audience.

Not to be outdone, Griswold replied, to more laughter, "Yes, Mr. Justice, and we are, of course, fully supporting the First Amendment." But, he noted, the First Amendment "was not intended to make it impossible for the Executive to function, or to protect the security of the United States."

Griswold again argued that the case had sped through the courts without adequate review. "Everything about this case has been frantic," he said.

In the short time he had left, Griswold asked the Court to order the lower court to review the evidence. The Court, he said, should use a standard that would stop publication of material that would "affect the security of the United States vitally over a long period."

Griswold ended his arguments, and the Court adjourned. The time, noted in the recording secretary's book, was 1:13 p.m.

seven
THE DECISION

FOR DAYS THE ATTORNEYS in the Pentagon Papers case had rushed from one court to another. When they weren't in court, they were poring over legal documents, preparing briefs, and preparing their arguments. Now all they could do was wait. For the next four days the whole nation waited while the justices sorted through what they had heard in court and the points made in the briefs.

To decide a case, the justices meet behind closed doors to discuss the issues, examine the briefs, consider the arguments, and review precedents that relate to the case. After the conference, they hold an initial vote. If the chief justice agrees with the majority, he writes the opinion or assigns it to one of the other justices on the same side. In cases where the chief justice votes with the minority, the justice who has served the longest and agrees with the majority makes the assignment.

The decision outlines the facts of the case and details the reasons behind the Court's ruling. Once the majority decision has been completed, the justices vote on it. The decision's author may add words or eliminate passages to win support from other justices. Those who agree with the final majority opinion will join it—that is, agree to put their names on it. These justices may also write their own opinion—called a concurring opinion—in which they state other reasons for supporting the majority vote.

Justices who vote against the majority opinion may write dissents that outline the reasons for their position.

Sometimes their arguments are so persuasive that they convince a majority of justices to join them. If that happens, the dissent becomes the majority opinion and the original majority opinion becomes a dissent. In a few instances, the Court cannot agree or wants additional information and decides to hold a second hearing on the case.

Writing an opinion may take several months. Because of the urgency of the Pentagon Papers case, the justices prepared their opinions in less than a week.

Occasionally, the Court issues an unsigned majority opinion. This is called a *per curiam* opinion, meaning one issued "by the court." Usually these are noncontroversial cases, and the decisions are generally unanimous and short.

Once the justices complete their voting, the Court announces its decision. In important cases, the chief justice or the author of the majority decision reads it to the public. It is then published and becomes the law of the land. Lawyers presenting similar cases will use the ruling as a basis for their arguments.

Deliberations

The justices decided to begin reviewing the case immediately after the arguments were heard on June 26. That afternoon they met to discuss the case. Chief Justice Burger wanted to hold more hearings on the case. He believed the government had not been given enough time to identify the documents that could damage national security.

Harlan, too, objected to the push to settle the case immediately. From the start, he had believed the case deserved lengthy and well-thought-out discussion and deliberation. Forced to vote now, he favored the government.

Blackmun voted with Burger, as he usually did.

Three justices—Black, Douglas, and Brennan—believed that the injunctions against the two newspapers should be lifted at once. Brennan concluded that only during a declared war could the government stop the presses. They voted to let the newspapers publish.

Justice Hugo L. Black believed that stopping publication of the Pentagon Papers was unacceptable.

Marshall and White believed that rather than trying to stop the presses, the government should have prosecuted the newspapers for disclosing classified material. The two justices voted against prior restraint in this case and for the newspapers.

Stewart had mixed views on the case. He sympathized with the government's need to keep certain information secret, and he believed that some material in the Pentagon Papers could cause harm to individual Americans. But he questioned whether the publication of the papers could cause immediate and irreparable harm to the nation. In the end, he decided the government had not proved that it could. He, too, voted for the newspapers. That made the vote six to three in favor of publication.

Usually, a justice voting in the majority is assigned to write the majority opinion. After researching the question carefully—sometimes a process that takes months—the justice writes the opinion and submits it to be reviewed by the other justices voting in the majority. They discuss their views at length and often add sections or compromise on wording before finally issuing the majority decision.

In this case, there simply was not time to do that. If the Court was going to lift the injunctions against the newspapers, it had to do it immediately or the decision would be meaningless. Instead of a lengthy majority opinion, the Court decided to issue a short *per curiam* decision that merely stated the outcome of the case and briefly mentioned the reasons behind it.

In addition, each justice would release a separate opinion—an extraordinary ten decisions in all, including the *per curiam* opinion. Not one of the nine opinions written by the justices gained support from more than three members of the Court.

court issues decision

On June 30, 1971, at 2:30 p.m., Chief Justice Warren Burger read the Court's decision to an eager crowd in the quiet courtroom. He had assigned himself this duty, even though it was customary for a member of the majority to read the decision.

By a 6 to 3 vote, the Supreme Court lifted the ban on *The New York Times* and the *Washington Post*. The justices reversed the Second Circuit's order for another hearing and upheld the District of Columbia Circuit's verdict in favor of the *Post*. The government, the Court ruled, had not met the "heavy burden" necessary for prior restraint. The press had won this battle.

KATHARINE GRAHAM, PUBLISHER OF THE *WASHINGTON POST*, AND BENJAMIN BRADLEE, EXECUTIVE EDITOR, SHARE A HAPPY MOMENT WHEN THEY HEAR THE SUPREME COURT'S DECISION PERMITTING THE *POST* AND THE *TIMES* TO CONTINUE PRINTING THE PENTAGON PAPERS.

THE JUSTICES OF THE SUPREME COURT WHO DECIDED THE PENTAGON PAPERS CASE. BACK ROW (L TO R): ASSOCIATE JUSTICES THURGOOD MARSHALL, POTTER STEWART, BYRON R. WHITE, AND HARRY A. BLACKMUN. FRONT ROW (L TO R): ASSOCIATE JUSTICES JOHN M. HARLAN, HUGO L. BLACK, CHIEF JUSTICE WARREN BURGER, AND ASSOCIATE JUSTICES WILLIAM O. DOUGLAS AND WILLIAM J. BRENNAN.

The decision was by no means simple or definitive. The one-page ruling, signed by no one, held that stopping the presses is almost always presumed to be unconstitutional. The government, it noted, "carries a heavy burden" to prove that such a step is justified. In the Pentagon Papers case, the decision concluded, the government had failed to meet that burden.

Concurring with the decision were Justices Black, Douglas, Marshall, Brennan, White, and Stewart. Chief Justice Burger and Justices Blackman and Harlan dissented.

Each of the nine justices filed his own opinion on the case. Even among those who supported the decision, there were varying interpretations of the First Amendment's relationship to national security. Justices Black and Douglas held that the First Amendment's guarantees were absolute. The amendment did not allow prior restraint of the press, they believed, and Congress could not abridge the amendment's guarantee of freedom of the press in any way.

On the other hand, Justices Brennan, Stewart, White, and Marshall asserted that the First Amendment's guarantees were not absolute. It was the Court's duty, they believed, to weigh competing concerns—in this case, freedom of the press versus national security—and decide which had the stronger claim.

In addition, Marshall discussed the concerns about separation of powers that Bickel had introduced in his arguments. Congress had passed laws making it a crime to publish certain documents (specifically those on how to build a hydrogen bomb). But in the Pentagon Papers case, he noted, Congress had never authorized the government to seek an injunction. Therefore, according to Marshall, the president did not have authority from Congress to stop the presses.

Nine Separate Opinions

The individual opinions ranged from Brennan's terse, three-page decision to White's ten-page dissent.

Justice Black's opinion, with Justice Douglas concurring, took the strongest view for freedom of the press. Black maintained that the Court should have lifted the restrictions against both newspapers even before the hearing. "Every moment's continuance of the injunctions against these newspapers amounts to a flagrant, indefensible, and continuing violation of the First Amendment," Black wrote. In a stinging rebuke of the justices who supported the government's case, Black said that their view—that sometimes the presses can be stopped—"would make a shambles of the First Amendment."

"For the first time in 182 years . . ." the justice continued, "the federal courts are asked to hold that the First Amendment does not mean what it says, but rather means that the Government can halt the publication of current news of vital importance to the people of this country."

The Founding Fathers created the Bill of Rights, he said, to "curtail and restrict" the powers of the three branches of government and to protect the people's rights, including freedom of the press. "Both the history and language of the First Amendment support the view that the press must be left free to publish news whatever the source, without censorship, injunctions, or prior restraints."

These leaders, Black wrote, protected the press in the First Amendment so that it could perform "its essential role in our democracy." That role, he said, was to "bare the secrets of government and inform the people," a task that could only be carried out by a "free and unrestricted press."

Perhaps the most important duty of the press, Black noted, was to stop government from "deceiving the people and sending them off to distant lands to die of foreign fevers and foreign shot and shell." Black commended *The New York Times* and the *Washington Post* for their "courageous reporting" in the Pentagon Papers case.

To allow the president "inherent power" to go to court in order to stop the presses in the name of national security, Black concluded, "would wipe out the First Amendment and destroy the fundamental liberty and security of the very people the Government hopes to make 'secure.'"

Justice Douglas's concurring opinion, joined by Justice Black, followed much the same arguments. Like Black, Douglas firmly believed that the wording of the First Amendment clearly prohibited governmental restraint of the press. In his opinion, he noted that Congress had defeated a proposed section of the Espionage Act that would have barred publication of military information during a war. Congress rejected the proposal because of concerns that it would violate the First Amendment.

The Pentagon Papers cases, Douglas said, would "go down in history as the most dramatic illustration" of governmental attempts to suppress embarrassing material. "Open debate and discussion of public issues are vital to our national health," Douglas concluded.

In a separate concurring opinion, Justice Brennan emphasized his opposition to prior restraints on the press. "The First Amendment stands as an absolute bar to the imposition of judicial restraints" in cases such as the

Pentagon Papers, he noted. He concluded that the courts should never have stopped the presses without indisputable government proof that publication would "inevitably, directly, and immediately cause" some catastrophic event.

Justice Stewart's opinion, joined by Justice White, stressed the importance of keeping in check the "enormous power" held by the president in military and foreign affairs. An informed public provided the only "effective restraint" upon such power, according to Stewart. And without "an informed and free press," he said, "there cannot be an enlightened people."

Stewart conceded that secrecy was required for national defense and international diplomacy. But, he contended, the responsibility for keeping secrets rested with the president, not with the press.

"If the Constitution gives the Executive a large degree of unshared power in the conduct of foreign affairs and the maintenance of our national defense, then under the Constitution, the Executive must have the largely unshared duty to determine and preserve the degree of internal security necessary to exercise that power successfully," Stewart wrote.

Keeping too many secrets undermined the effort to protect vital information, the justice said. "When everything is classified," he wrote, "then nothing is classified." An effective system, he added, disclosed as much as possible to maintain credibility.

Congress's role, Stewart said, was to pass criminal laws to protect government secrets. The courts shouldered the duty of deciding cases brought under those laws.

Stewart said he was convinced that some of the documents among the Pentagon Papers should not be published. But, he said, the government had failed to prove that making the documents public would cause "direct, immediate, and irreparable damage" to the nation. Therefore, he concluded, the First Amendment required the Court to lift the ban on the press.

Justice White cited the Constitution's "extraordinary protection against prior restraints" in his concurring opinion, which Justice Stewart joined. Unlike Black and Douglas, White believed the First Amendment allowed stop-the-press orders in certain cases. He also believed, like Stewart, that release of the Pentagon Papers documents would cause "substantial damage to public interests." Nevertheless, he opposed a ban on publication because he did not think the government had met the "very heavy burden that it must meet to warrant an injunction." Without a law from Congress allowing such restraints on the press, White said, the president did not have the authority to ask the Court to bar publication.

He noted that "a responsible press" might choose never to publish the "more sensitive" materials, but the Court should not impose that choice on a free press. He also noted that if members of the press did publish the material, the government could file criminal charges against them. White warned the press that he "would have no difficulty" voting to convict such violators.

In yet another separate, concurring opinion, Justice Marshall focused on "whether this Court or the Congress has the power to make law." Marshall concluded that Congress alone held that power, and Congress had already rejected laws that would have allowed press censorship during wartime.

"The Constitution provides that Congress shall make laws, the President execute laws, and courts interpret laws," Marshall wrote. To allow the government to censor the press in the Pentagon Papers case, Marshall concluded, would give too much power to the president and interfere with the separation of powers required by the Constitution.

THE DISSENTERS

The three dissenting justices issued their own separate opinions. Chief Justice Burger, in his opinion, criticized what he called the "unseemly haste" of the Court in deciding the case. Because of the "hectic pressures" created by the fast-paced court proceedings, Burger contended that the judges did not know the facts of the case. "The haste precluded reasonable and deliberate judicial treatment of these cases," he wrote, "and was not warranted."

He rejected Black's view that the First Amendment never allowed prior restraint of the press. With proper review, he said, the Pentagon Papers case might have revealed a situation which called for a press ban. He also noted that the *Times* itself had held the papers for three months before publishing. A further delay, according to Burger, would not have threatened the public's right to know.

Burger suggested a more reasonable approach would have been for the *Times* to allow the government to review the papers and determine which could be safely published. He said every citizen is duty bound to turn over stolen property or secret government documents. "This duty rests on taxi drivers, Justices, and *The New York Times*," he noted.

Justice Harlan also issued a dissent, joined by the chief justice and Justice Blackmun. He, too, decried the "frenzied train of events" in which the decision was made. Given the rushed schedule, Harlan based his dissent on the need for separation of powers. Because the Constitution gave the president the power to manage foreign affairs, Harlan wrote, the Court did not have the power to override the president's efforts to do his job.

"I cannot believe," he concluded, "that the doctrine prohibiting prior restraints reaches to the point of preventing courts from maintaining the *status quo* long enough to act responsibly in matters of such national importance as those involved here."

In his dissent, Justice Blackmun said all but the eleven items on the government's list could be published as far as he was concerned. But he agreed with U.S. Circuit Court Judge Wilkey's assessment that some of the information on the list could harm the nation if made public. Urging the two newspapers to "be fully aware of their ultimate responsibilities to the United States of America," Blackmun noted that if the sensitive documents were published and prolonged the war or delayed the freeing of U.S. prisoners, "then the Nation's people will know where the responsibility for these sad consequences rests."

eIGHT
Aftermath

Cheers Broke Out in the newsrooms of the *Washington Post* and *The New York Times* as soon as the decision was announced. *Times* publisher Sulzberger reacted with "complete joy and delight" at the news. "I never really doubted that this day would come and that we'd win," he said at a press conference called shortly after Burger's June 30 reading of the decision.

Times managing editor A. M. Rosenthal said the Pentagon Papers case had shown people "that a great deal of information is classified for no real national security interest." He said he thought the case would open more information to the press and the public. The Pentagon Papers, he told reporters, "are a matter of enormous historical interest."

At the *Washington Post*, publisher Katharine Graham said, "We are extremely gratified not only from the point of view of newspapers . . . but gratified from the point of view of government, and the public's right to know."

Newspaper officials rejected Chief Justice Warren Burger's suggestion that the government be allowed to review the documents before they were printed. They said such a process would amount to "unconstitutional censorship."

The *Times* published the remaining articles in the series as planned following the decision. Other newspapers, including the *Post*, continued with their own articles. The following month, the *Times* published a book on

PREPARED PAGE OF THE PENTAGON PAPERS SERIES IS WHEELED FROM A GUARDED STORAGE AREA INTO THE COMPOSING ROOM OF *THE NEW YORK TIMES*.

the Pentagon Papers that included the *Times* series, the Supreme Court decision, and about 5 percent of the documents in the original study. The book was a best seller, with more than a million copies sold.

The United States government issued its own book on the Pentagon Papers on September 27. It filled twelve volumes and included many of the documents once classified top secret.

The day before the Supreme Court's decision, Senator Mike Gravel, D-Alaska, entered his copy of the Pentagon Papers into the official record of his Senate subcommittee on building and grounds. The Gravel version contained 4,100 pages of documents. He said he took the action in his role as senator communicating with his constituents. Beacon Press, the publishing sector of the Unitarian Universalist Church, eventually published the documents in a book released on October 22, 1971. The Beacon Press version of the Pentagon Papers was a five-volume set that contained many documents not included in the government edition.

None of the book versions included material from the four volumes on diplomacy.

CONGRESS AND THE PENTAGON PAPERS

Beginning on June 23, 1971, a congressional subcommittee on foreign operations and government information held

THE PUBLISHING
OF THE PENTAGON PAPERS

The story leading up to the publishing of the Pentagon Papers reads like a thriller, with midnight meetings, threats, and sacrifice.

It began with Daniel Ellsberg, who secretly photocopied the Pentagon report and leaked it to *The New York Times* after leaders in Congress refused to make the papers public. When the courts stopped the *Times* from publishing its series on the Pentagon Papers, Ellsberg—now on the run—gave a copy of the papers to Ben Bagdikian of the *Washington Post*. After the courts issued an injunction against the *Post* as well, Bagdikian—at Ellsberg's urging—passed the papers to the junior senator from Alaska, Democrat Mike Gravel.

In 1969, during his first year as a senator, Gravel had visited Vietnam. The trip convinced him that the war was immoral and that United States attempts to win the conflict were futile. Gravel was leading efforts to end the draft of young American men when someone telephoned him and asked if he would read the Pentagon Papers into the Congressional Record. He said he would. Shortly afterward, at midnight, Gravel pulled his car up in front of the Mayflower Hotel in Washington, D.C. Bagdikian walked over, opened the trunk, and threw in a stack of papers. Both men quickly drove away. The copy Gravel received contained 4,100 pages of the 7,000-page Pentagon study.

Gravel tried several times to read the Pentagon Papers during debate in the Senate, but other senators shouted him down. On June 29, the day before the Supreme Court ruled in the Pentagon Papers case, Senator Gravel called a special session of his subcommittee on public buildings and grounds. He read aloud several sections of the Pentagon Papers. Gravel then entered the entire 4,100 pages of his copy into the subcommittee's official record. The chair of the full committee refused to publish the document.

That led Gravel to seek a private publisher for the papers.

Even though the Supreme Court ruling on June 3o allowed newspapers to continue their series on the Pentagon Papers, the news reports contained only a small number of excerpts and a few original documents from the Pentagon study. Gravel believed the entire report should be published. He asked his assistant, Leonard Rodberg, to help him edit the report and assemble it for submission to publishers.

After talking with thirty-five publishers and being rejected by all of them, Gravel contacted Beacon Press. A small, non-profit, Boston publishing house, Beacon Press served as the publishing arm of a religious group, the Unitarian Universalist Association (UUA). The Unitarians had long been involved in liberal political activism, including civil rights, abortion, and the black power movement. In 1961, the group had joined with Universalists to form the UUA. For a decade the association had opposed the Vietnam War.

When Gobin Stair, Beacon Press director, began reading Gravel's stack of papers, it didn't impress him as best-seller material. "It was a boring book," he recalled. "It went on and on and on with these details." His editor, however, argued that the Pentagon report was important and that alone would make it a book people would read.

Stair still hadn't decided whether to publish the report when he got a late-night telephone call at home from President Richard Nixon. It quickly became clear that Nixon was pressuring him not to publish the Pentagon Papers. That settled the matter for Stair. "To be told by Nixon . . . not to do it, convinced me before I had [completely] decided, that it was a book to do," he later recalled.

Stair took his proposal to UUA president Robert N. West. The two men and executive vice president Raymond Hopkins met in the president's Boston office on a summer day in late July or early August 1971 to discuss the matter.

Publishing the papers certainly fit in with the church's longstanding opposition to the Vietnam War. Printing the study, however, would require five bulky volumes and would cost approximately $50,000, according to Stair. West favored publishing, but he knew the cost might tax the church's finances. West and Stair turned to Hopkins, who dealt with fiscal affairs for the church. Hopkins assured the men that, in his opinion, the book would make money. "I told them, 'Every library in the country would have to have a copy,'" Hopkins recalled. Reassured, West gave Stair the go-ahead to publish. Everyone in the room knew the decision would lead to trouble from the Nixon administration. They didn't guess, however, that it would end up costing Beacon Press almost a quarter of a million dollars in legal fees and unsold books.

In August, Stair announced that Beacon Press would publish the Mike Gravel edition of the Pentagon Papers. The report was published in four volumes on October 22, 1971.

A fifth volume was published six months later. Almost immediately, the Nixon administration set about to block sales and to harass the church. Within days, FBI agents appeared at the UUA's bank and began searching the church's financial records. As part of their search, the agents recorded the name of every contributor to the church.

The FBI also ordered Stair to appear before a federal grand jury to testify about Beacon Press's publication of the classified report. Gravel claimed that the Constitution's guarantee of free speech and the immunity provided members of Congress protected Rodberg, his aide (who had also been subpoenaed), from court action and that Rodberg could not be made to testify. The case traveled all the way to the Supreme Court. On June 29, 1972, the Court ruled that Rodberg could not be made to testify about legislative acts. But, it said, the publishing of the Pentagon Papers by a private firm was not considered a legislative act. Therefore, the Court sent the case back to the grand jury, with instructions that Rodberg could be questioned about the case. The decision later served as a basis for the Court's ruling in 1974 ordering the release of the Nixon tapes, a move that eventually led to the president's resignation.

Twelve days before the ruling in the Gravel case, Nixon's Plumbers unit was arrested for breaking into the Democratic National Committee offices. The arrest and subsequent Watergate scandals shifted attention away from the Pentagon Papers, and the federal government dropped the case against Beacon Press and Rodberg.

Although Beacon Press was relieved not to have to pursue the case further, UUA's legal fees approached $225,000. First Amendment champion Alan Dershowitz volunteered his legal expertise, but other lawyers' fees and court expenses mounted during the eight-month-long court battle. In addition, the court actions delayed distribution, and when the books were finally released, the volumes did not sell. "I don't think we sold eight copies [of the books] to eight libraries," said Hopkins. He guessed that libraries did not want to risk prosecution by the federal government for possessing classified documents. Hopkins noted that he "read and read and read" the books and never found any information that should have been classified in the first place.

Hopkins believed that the Nixon administration knew it would ultimately lose a court fight against free speech. "That's why they [Nixon's men] were so aggressive in bullying us." During the time he worked with the UUA, he said, his mail was censored and his phones were tapped. Though he never tried to prove the allegation, he said he "ended my phone conversations with a message to the FBI or the CIA." Hopkins regretted the money lost in the battle, but he said he would still have recommended that Beacon publish the papers. "I was proud to be a part of it," he added.

Despite the great financial cost, Beacon Press and the UUA never regretted its courageous stand for free speech.

Shortly after Stair announced Beacon would publish the volumes, an editorial in the UUA magazine *Unitarian Universalist World* asked the question: "Why should the UU press take the risks and become involved in the most vicious battle for the free press since the Zenger trial?" The answer: "For the simple reason that freedom from bureaucratic censorship is one of the objectives of this denomination and of the press which represents it."

hearings on the government's classification system and the Pentagon Papers case. But the discussions led nowhere. No action was taken, no vote passed on changes to the system. The Pentagon Papers did spark heated discussion about past leaders' roles in the Vietnam War. Many pointed to the massive study as proof that officials knowingly undertook policies they knew would not succeed in ending the war. "Our Presidents did not stumble step by step into Vietnam, unaware of the quagmire," wrote Leslie Gelb, the former Defense Department worker who directed the Pentagon Papers project, in a guest column in *The New York Times.* "U.S. involvement did not stem from a failure to foresee consequences. Vietnam was indeed a quagmire, but most of our leaders knew it."

Others, however, clung to the view that America's leaders were misled, just as the public had been. Historian Arthur Schlesinger argued that the Vietnam War "was marked much more by ignorance, misjudgment, and muddle than by foresight, awareness, and calculation."

Embroiled in the Watergate scandal that came to light the following year, Congress never held hearings on the content of the Pentagon Papers or the failed Vietnam policies they revealed.

REACTION FROM THE WHITE HOUSE: A "CONSPIRACY"

The president's men took two different approaches in their public response to the Pentagon Papers decision. Adopting a "tough-guy" stance, Attorney General Mitchell warned that the government would file criminal charges against publishers who violated the law in making the Pentagon Papers public. Secretary of State Rogers used a gentler argument. He told reporters he hoped newspapers would realize their obligation not to publish the sections of the study that could damage national security. He added that the government would soon identify which parts would be harmful.

Secretary of Defense Laird suggested the White House

release the entire study to the press, since the media had agreed to delete any sensitive material. National security adviser Kissinger vehemently opposed the move. He argued that the White House must uphold the principle of government security. In the end, the government's version of the Pentagon Papers published in September contained many blacked-out areas of subjects considered too sensitive to be revealed. The Nixon administration did not file criminal charges against the newspapers, but it did file suit against Beacon Press for its publication of the papers. The charges were later dropped.

On July 1, 1971, as the newspapers celebrated the Supreme Court decision, Nixon, Haldeman, and Kissinger conferred privately on their next step. The whole episode had angered Nixon. The Court's decision enraged him. "We're up against an enemy, a conspiracy," Nixon told his advisers on July 1. "They're using any means. We are going to use any means. Is that clear?"

The first acts taken in the president's campaign against the "enemy" focused on Daniel Ellsberg. From the time he learned of Ellsberg's involvement, Nixon had directed his rage against the man he viewed as a traitor. His need to discredit Ellsberg and other antiwar critics consumed him, as did the desire to plug the leaks to the press. Nixon became increasingly concerned that Ellsberg or others would release other sensitive information. He vowed to "destroy" Ellsberg in the press.

Ultimately, the president's efforts to "get" Ellsberg went far beyond smearing him in the newspapers. On July 17, Nixon's aide Ehrlichman set up a group to investigate security leaks. Because of their assignment to plug leaks, the group soon became known as the Plumbers unit. Former CIA agent E. Howard Hunt and former FBI agent G. Gordon Liddy were among those on the team.

Headed by a young White House lawyer named Egil "Bud" Krogh, on Labor Day weekend in 1971 the team broke into the office of Ellsberg's psychiatrist, Lewis

Fielding, in search of records that might incriminate Ellsberg. They left the office a shambles, but evidently failed to find information discrediting Ellsberg. Although Nixon later claimed that he did not order the illegal break-in or know about it, White House tapes revealed that the president had tried to cover up his connection with the Plumbers unit.

ELLSBERG ON TRIAL

After months of delays, the trial of Ellsberg and Russo began in U.S. District Court in January 1973. As the trial progressed, a pattern of "dirty tricks" ordered or endorsed by the Nixon White House emerged. Among them were illegal wiretaps of Ellsberg's telephone and the break-in at the office of Ellsberg's psychiatrist. Later charges implicated the White House in ordering twelve Cuban Americans "to totally incapacitate" Ellsberg. The assault was planned for May 3, 1972, but was never carried out. Ellsberg later said the Watergate special prosecutor told him the

ON MAY 11, 1973, ALL CHARGES AGAINST ANTHONY RUSSO (RIGHT) AND DANIEL ELLSBERG (AT MICROPHONE) WERE DISMISSED.

Cubans revealed the plot while giving testimony during the Watergate investigations.

On June 17, 1972, almost a year after the Supreme Court decision on the Pentagon Papers case, five men later identified as members of Nixon's Plumbers unit were arrested while trying to tap the phones inside the Democratic National Committee offices at the Watergate hotel and office complex in Washington, D.C.

These revelations, some of which came to light during the trial, led the court to dismiss all charges against Ellsberg and Russo. On May 11, 1973, the eighty-ninth day of the trial, the judge threw out the case. In making the ruling, Judge William M. Byrne Jr. berated the federal government for "improper government conduct shielded so long from public view." In harsh tones, the judge told the packed courtroom that the actions of the administration were so appalling that they "offend the sense of justice."

In his memoirs, Nixon admitted that he might have known about the break-in after it occurred. But he added, "I do not accept, that it [the break-in] was as wrong or excessive as what Daniel Ellsberg did, and I still believe that it is a tragedy of circumstances that Bud Krogh and John Ehrlichman went to jail and Daniel Ellsberg went free."

watergate scandal

The *Washington Post*, and later *The New York Times* and other newspapers, tracked the "dirty tricks" against Ellsberg and the Democrats back to Nixon and top officials in his administration. During televised hearings by the Senate Watergate Committee in the spring and summer of 1973, Nixon aide John Dean described criminal acts, hush money, and a massive cover-up at the White House. The discovery of a taping system in the Oval Office that recorded Nixon's conversations signaled the beginning of the end for the president. On July 27, 1974, the House Judiciary

PRESIDENTIAL ADVISER HENRY KISSINGER (R) AND HANOI'S LE DUC THO SHAKE HANDS AFTER A MEETING ON THE VIETNAM PEACE AGREEMENT.

Committee approved the first of three articles of impeachment against Nixon, charging the president with obstruction of justice. To avoid an impeachment trial, Nixon resigned on August 8, the only U.S. president to do so.

VIETNAM WAR WINDS DOWN

In January 1972, Nixon announced that 70,000 troops would be pulled out of Vietnam by May of that year. In June, after tens of thousands of North Vietnamese soldiers entered South Vietnam, the United States withdrew all but 60,000 technicians and advisers. U.S. air forces also remained in the area. That December, Americans launched a twelve-day bombing assault on North Vietnam, pausing only on Christmas Day.

Throughout this period, Henry Kissinger negotiated in secret with the North Vietnamese and the Viet Cong. In January 1973, representatives from the three parties signed the Paris Peace Agreement, which called for the complete withdrawal of American forces. In exchange, the North

Vietnamese agreed to release U.S. prisoners of war (POWs) by April. By August, all American military operations had ceased, and the last remaining U.S. troops withdrew from the country. On April 29, 1975, in a dramatic rescue operation, U.S. helicopters evacuated American and South Vietnamese civilians from the U.S. embassy in Saigon as the Viet Cong took over the country. Vietnam today operates under communist rule. More than 58,000 Americans and an estimated 5 million Vietnamese died in the war. Almost one million soldiers from both sides were wounded during the hostilities.

Ellsberg theorizes that the Vietnam War would have lasted at least two years longer than it did if Nixon had not been forced to resign. The president's resignation in part resulted from Nixon's role in ordering illegal acts against Ellsberg to silence him, so indirectly the Pentagon Papers did help end the war, he believes.

"I believe that if he [Nixon] had not felt a compulsion to commit such crimes against me," Ellsberg told a CNN interviewer, "he would not have been vulnerable to prosecution himself and would not have had to leave office and therefore, he would have continued the war."

Lessons Learned

In the aftermath of the Pentagon Papers case, the Supreme Court has upheld the right of the press to publish a wide variety of material. The 1988 Supreme Court case, *Hustler Magazine, Inc.* v. *Falwell*, established the right to parody public figures. The Court's ruling said the First Amendment protects satire, even when it is outrageous. Conservative minister Jerry Falwell sued Larry Flynt after the publisher of the sex-oriented magazine *Hustler* printed a lewd parody of Falwell. The Court, in its unanimous decision, ruled that the press must be given "breathing space" to practice its First Amendment freedom.

In other cases, the Supreme Court has struck down laws that punished the press for publishing information on secret judicial misconduct hearings, rape victims' names, the names of juvenile offenders, and editorials supporting a particular issue on election day. Still, the verdict continues to be mixed when the material printed involves military information. Congress has passed laws that make it illegal to publish certain types of information. Some of those laws remain in place. Other laws have been negated by actions taken by people or entities not directly involved in a case, as happened in 1979 when the federal government prevented *The Progressive* magazine from publishing an article on how to construct a hydrogen bomb. Under the Atomic Energy Act, passed by Congress in 1954, the government could keep secret any information related to the construction of nuclear weapons. The federal court granted the government's request for a prior restraint order, saying that the article, if published, would cause "direct, immediate and irreparable damage to the United States." The case never reached the Supreme Court. The government dropped its suit against the magazine and author Howard Morland after the *Sacramento Bee* published the bomb instructions in a twelve-page letter to the editor. *The Progressive* then published its story in November 1979.

The Progressive's managing editor, Sam Day, later said he published the story to boost opposition to nuclear weapons. Government officials at the time warned that the article's publication would allow foreign countries to produce their own bombs. Later study revealed that the story did neither: No other country used the H-bomb technology to produce weapons, but the American people did not adopt an antinuclear stance.

In a 1985 case, Samuel Loring Morison became the first person ever to be convicted for leaking classified defense documents to the press. Morison, a naval analyst, turned over a classified photograph of a Soviet nuclear carrier to *Jane's Defence Weekly*, an internationally recognized magazine focused on military issues and published in Great Britain. After the weekly published the photo, Morison was charged under the 1917 Espionage Act. The Supreme Court declined to consider his appeal, and in 1988 he began serving a two-year jail sentence for the crime. The case sparked outrage from the press, which charged that the Morison arrest would severely discourage people from leaking information that the public should see. On his last day in office, January 20, 2001, President William J. Clinton pardoned Morison, long after he had served his sentence. A pardon lifts restrictions placed on a convicted felon that prevent him or her from voting, holding public office, and being eligible for certain jobs.

More than thirty years after *The New York Times* published the Pentagon Papers, the resultant court case stands as a primer on the First Amendment. The ruling reiterated and strengthened the doctrine that prior restraint is almost never allowed under the Constitution. Only when publication would cause direct and immediate damage to the nation can the government stop the presses.

In addition, the case helped define and further guarantee the role of a free press in a democracy. That role, today as in the days of the American Revolution, is to expose government wrongdoing and keep the public informed about abuses of power. While the First Amendment does not force the government to release material to the public, it guarantees the press the right to reveal such information.

After the Pentagon Papers episode, Congress took steps to give the press—and the public—the tools to obtain that information from the government. New laws amended the Freedom of Information Act to make it easier to view classified material. But recent efforts by political leaders have threatened to reverse those gains. In 2000 President Clinton vetoed a congressional bill that would have made it a crime to leak government information to the news media. Such leaks are still legal.

In the words of former *Post* publisher Graham, the Pentagon Papers "laid bare . . . precisely the process by which most of the business of government is carried forward." But whether that revelation will have any lasting effect, she said, depends on the government's willingness to operate in the open—and the public's vigilance in making sure that happens.

USA PATRIOT ACT: THREAT TO LIBERTY OR ANTITERRORIST TOOL?

After terrorists attacked the World Trade Center and the Pentagon on September 11, 2001, President George W. Bush pushed for passage of the USA Patriot Act. The bill, signed on October 26, 2001, put in place new regulations that have tightened government secrecy, dramatically expanded federal search and surveillance powers, and eliminated many of the checks that helped ensure against government abuse of power. Under the act, the federal government can require businesses, libraries, and individual Americans to turn over the personal records of clients and customers. These include reports on what a person buys, sells, and reads; his or her financial records, medical histories, and business dealings; and computer records of e-mails, Internet sites visited, and other computer uses. The law requires businesses and others to keep secret the government's demand for information. Unlike other searches, no court approval is required. The government does not have to produce any evidence of criminal acts or even suspicious behavior in order to search a person's records.

Critics charge that the Bush administration has used the fear of terrorists as well as the fear of appearing to be a disloyal American to quash opposition and keep government operations secret. "As apprehension of subversives rose, so did the scope of government secrecy," said John Podesta, former chief of staff to President Bill Clinton, during a speech at Princeton University in March 2004.

"Each time our nation faces a threat to national security there is a powerful tension between the need to keep the peo-

THE DEBATE CONTINUES. HERE, BUSH ADMINISTRATION ATTORNEY GENERAL JOHN ASHCROFT DEFENDS THE USA PATRIOT ACT, WHICH SOME BELIEVE STIFLES FREE SPEECH AND CIVIL LIBERTIES.

ple informed and the need to keep the enemy in the dark." He noted, however, that history has shown that "excessive secrecy does not lead to improved national security. Just the opposite has proved true." There are some things the government needs to keep secret, Podesta conceded, but "a culture of secrecy," he pointed out, "has led to regrettable policy choices, wasted resources and a decline in public trust."

Critics in Congress have called for amendments to the act that would put limits on federal powers. Key sections of the bill—including those that allow police to spy on Internet usage and reading material without a warrant—are due to expire on December 31, 2005. Other sections have no expiration date.

In his state of the union speech on January 20, 2004, President Bush called for Congress to renew the USA Patriot Act. The Bush administration and its supporters contend that the act and government secrets are essential tools in the war against terrorism. Attorney General John Ashcroft has charged that critics of such policies "give ammunition to America's enemies and pause to America's friends."

As part of the administration's campaign against terrorism, Ashcroft ordered courts to close immigration court hearings. Claiming national security concerns, the Bush administration refused to allow the press to cover the hearings. The *Detroit Free Press* filed suit, and the U.S. appeals court sided with the newspaper. Noting that "democracies die behind closed doors," the court ordered the government to open the hearings. The case may be headed for the Supreme Court for a final ruling.

Ashcroft has pledged a "comprehensive, coordinated, Government-wide, aggressive, properly resourced, and sustained effort" to fight "the problem of unauthorized disclosures." In March 2003, President Bush delayed for three years the release of millions of government documents. The presidential order also gave federal agencies new authority to keep "national security" information under lock and key indefinitely.

Ashcroft's goal is to stop leaks of information the Bush administration does not want made public—unclassified material as well as classified. This, say critics, amounts to an unofficial secrets act not approved by Congress.

First Amendment advocates decry such constraints on the press and civil liberties. Expanding the type of documents that can be classified, they believe, is just another attempt to keep information from the American public. A task force studying the government's classification system in 1970 made the surprising recommendation to eliminate the system altogether rather than keep secret information that researchers and scientists could use to good advantage. Short of that, the task force proposed a system in which documents would automatically be made public after five years. It concluded that up to 90 percent of the classified documents on scientific and technical matters did not need to be kept secret. Congress, however, took no action on the recommendations.

Among the critics of increased classification is the very man who argued more than three decades ago that the Supreme Court should keep the government's secrets. Erwin N. Griswold, who as Nixon's solicitor general argued for the government in the Pentagon Papers case, said in 1989 that the publication of the top secret documents never harmed the nation.

"I have never seen any trace of a threat to the national security from the publication [of the Pentagon Papers]," he said. "Indeed, I have never seen it even suggested that there was such an actual threat."

Government officials classify massive amounts of material not because of concerns over national security but rather to prevent "governmental embarrassment of one sort or another," Griswold said. "There is very rarely any real risk to current national security from the publication of facts relating to transactions in the past [apart from documents that detail weapons systems], even the fairly recent past. This is the lesson of the Pentagon Papers."

During a 1971 interview with Walter Cronkite, Ellsberg, the man whose actions set off the events that led to the Pentagon Papers case, expressed his own views on the lessons learned:

> I think the lesson is that the people of this country can't afford to let the President run the country by himself, the foreign affairs any more than domestic affairs, without the help of the Congress, without the help of the public.

Adds Sanford Ungar, former *Washington Post* reporter and author of *The Papers & The Papers: An Account of the Legal and Political Battle Over the Pentagon Papers*:

> The lesson in the case was that you cannot always take the word of the government as to what is damaging to national security: government officials have a universal instinct to protect themselves and to define national security as whatever is consistent with their personal or bureaucratic interest at any given time.

Ungar said that officials today continue in their efforts to keep government operations secret, especially after terrorist attacks on the Pentagon and the World Trade Center and the war on Iraq.

"In moments of crisis, we must be even more cautious about the surrender of civil liberties to government," Ungar warns. "It is very easy in a time of crisis for citizens to say to the government, 'Here, take all this power. Protect us. Do whatever you need to do.'" But when citizens give up their responsibility to oversee government, it opens the door to abuse of power. And, says Ungar, it takes a long time to recover from such abuses.

APPENDIX
THE VIETNAM WAR

According to the Pentagon Papers, American politicians realized early on that the United States could not win the war in Vietnam. Instead of pulling out, however, they continued the conflict to force the enemy to accept peace terms favorable to the United States. In the end, this strategy failed, too, and Ho Chi Minh and the communists took control.

The U.S. Congress never declared war on Vietnam. But the war raged on, nevertheless. By the time it ended with the fall of South Vietnam in 1975, the conflict had claimed the lives of 58,200 American soldiers. Of the 2.7 million U.S. veterans who served in the Vietnam War, more than 300,000 were wounded, and about 75,000 suffered permanent disabilities. About 1,300 are still listed as missing in action. During the three decades the United States was involved in the territory, American administrations from Truman to Ford spent more than $150 billion in Vietnam.

The toll on Vietnam was far greater. The hostilities that ravaged the country from 1954 to 1975 claimed the lives of an estimated 4 million civilian men, women, and children in the north and the south, according to some accounts. Some 1.1 million soldiers died, and another 600,000 were wounded. Almost one of every ten Vietnamese citizens died or was wounded during the struggle. Twenty million gallons of Agent Orange, a plant poison that destroyed vegetation, and other herbicides were sprayed along areas where Viet Cong soldiers hid. Today an estimated one million Vietnamese citizens suffer from cancers or deformities because of exposure to the poisonous chemicals used during the war, according to scientists at a 2002 Yale conference on Vietnam and Agent Orange. American soldiers developed similar health problems linked to the poisons.

The chemicals also destroyed large sections of Vietnam's mangrove forests, which still have not grown back more than thirty years later. This has resulted in erosion and the loss of birds, fish, and animals. Some species have become extinct. The environmental damage caused by the war may take many decades to repair, according to a scientific study on the country's ecology.

The U.S. war in Vietnam was triggered not by a dramatic attack like Pearl Harbor but by a gradual buildup of American interests in the region. Presidents sent advisers, then money, then bombers, then troops to Vietnam.

In the 1940s, the Vietnamese were embroiled in a dispute with the French over control of the region. After talks with the French broke down in 1946, the Vietnamese forces under Ho Chi Minh (the Vietminh) attacked French troops, launching the Indochina War.

By the late 1940s, the Vietminh, allied with Communist China and the Soviet Union, controlled the north. Anticommunist forces backed by the French strengthened their control of the south.

In 1950 U.S. President Harry S. Truman sent military advisers to the region and pledged $15 million to the French war effort. President Dwight D. Eisenhower stepped further into the quagmire in 1954 when he justified U.S. presence in Vietnam by setting forth the domino theory:

"You have a row of dominoes set up. You knock over the first one, and what will happen to the last one is the certainty that it will go over very quickly."

By early May of 1954 the French had had enough of the conflict and began to withdraw troops. The 1954 Geneva Convention Agreements that followed called for a ceasefire and temporarily divided the country into North and South

Vietnam until national elections could be held in 1956. South Vietnamese leaders refused to sign the agreement or to hold elections. The following year, in a rigged election, U.S.-backed Ngo Dinh Diem assumed power in South Vietnam. By 1956, the last French troops had withdrawn from the conflict. In response, Eisenhower sent in a team of American advisers to train South Vietnamese soldiers. As the Cold War between the communist Soviet Union and the United States intensified, North Vietnamese forces followed the Ho Chi Minh Trail into South Vietnam. In July 1959, during a strike near Saigon, the capital of South Vietnam, two U.S. military advisers lost their lives—the first Americans killed during the war.

At decade's end, a special band of South Vietnamese soldiers called the Viet Cong joined forces with North Vietnamese troops. President John F. Kennedy, the third president to deal with the Vietnam issue, increased American involvement in the early 1960s. Under his administration, the United States sent more than 16,000 military advisers to Vietnam, spent $400 million in military aid, and began using Agent Orange. In early November 1963 Diem was assassinated in a military takeover by South Vietnamese generals. Kennedy supported the ouster, though apparently not the murder of Diem. The president's decision to back the coup tied the United States more firmly to South Vietnam and its fate.

After Kennedy was assassinated on November 22, 1963, President Lyndon B. Johnson took on the burden of running the war. South Vietnam military men jockeyed for power. The unstable government made it difficult for South Vietnam to wage war successfully against the north. As a result, Johnson greatly increased the number of American troops sent to fight in Vietnam.

In August 1964, North Vietnamese torpedo boats fired on a U.S. destroyer in international waters in the Tonkin Gulf off the coast of North Vietnam. Of two incidents reported, one never occurred and one was in response to U.S. spy activities. However, Johnson used the incidents to convince Congress to allow him to wage an undeclared war in Vietnam. The Gulf of Tonkin Resolution, approved on August 7, gave Johnson the authority to "take all necessary measures to repel any armed attack against the forces of the United States and to prevent further aggression."

"Operation Rolling Thunder" began in March 1965, with U.S. bombing raids directed at North Vietnamese. The bombing would continue for three years. The first American combat troops arrived in Vietnam later that year. By the end of 1968, more than 500,000 American soldiers were involved in the war.

During the Vietnamese Tet holiday in January 1968, North Vietnamese and Viet Cong forces seized control of several cities in the south. They were soon driven back by American soldiers in a major defeat of the communist forces. But their initial success during the Tet Offensive showed Americans that the war would not be easily won.

Meanwhile, more and more Americans opposed the war. A growing number of students, veterans from earlier wars, movie stars, and ordinary Americans protested at antiwar rallies. Black civil rights leader Martin Luther King Jr. called for an end to the hostilities. Young men burned draft cards and fled to Canada or served time in jail rather than fight in Vietnam. Faced with growing opposition because of his war policies, President Johnson announced in March 1968 that he would not run for reelection. He called for peace talks between the United States and North Vietnam, which began in May but soon came to a standstill. Finally, in November, the United States stopped its bombing raids in North Vietnam, and in January 1969 South Vietnam and the Viet Cong joined the peace talks.

Shortly after taking office in January 1969, President Richard M. Nixon ordered secret bombing in Cambodia, where North Vietnamese troops had camps and supplies. Nixon extended the bombing to Laos in 1970. Peace talks stalled.

Americans reacted with disgust when they learned in 1969 that U.S. soldiers had slaughtered villagers at My Lai in March 1968. Public outrage against the war intensified in May 1970 after National Guardsmen shot and killed four protesting students and wounded nine others at Kent State University in Ohio.

Nixon began shifting the burden of fighting the war to South Vietnamese soldiers, a process dubbed "Vietnamization." By the end of 1971, U.S. troops had been reduced to fewer than 200,000.

In June 1971, *The New York Times* printed the first of a ten-part series on the Pentagon Papers, a classified history of the Vietnam War. Although the study revealed deception and mismanagement of the war by U.S. officials, the extensive report had no immediate effect on the conflict or on public opinion. The incident did, however, spur Nixon to take illegal actions against the man who leaked the study. Nixon's failed attempt to cover up those and similar activities ultimately led to his resignation.

Before his downfall, the president sold himself to the voters as the candidate who would bring peace in Vietnam. Henry Kissinger, Nixon's national security adviser, revealed in 1972 that he and North Vietnamese leader Le Duc Tho had been involved in secret negotiations since 1970. When the North Vietnamese refused to meet American demands, however, Nixon ordered massive bombing of military and civilian targets in North Vietnam. In doing so, Nixon followed the same failed policies of other presidents as revealed in the Pentagon Papers. The bombings caused a resurgence of antiwar protests in the United States and elsewhere.

Shortly before the 1972 election, Kissinger announced, "Peace is at hand." South Vietnam, however, refused to go along with agreements made between the United States and North Vietnam. Finally, all four parties—the United States, North Vietnam, the Viet Cong, and South Vietnam—signed a cease-fire agreement on January 27, 1973. By March, all American ground troops had left the country. The secret bombing of Cambodia stopped in August, after Congress learned of the raids and ordered an end to them.

PRESIDENT RICHARD M. NIXON BIDS AN EMOTIONAL FAREWELL TO HIS STAFF AND CABINET AFTER RESIGNING FROM OFFICE. HIS WIFE, PAT, AND DAUGHTER PATRICIA STAND AT HIS SIDE.

Despite the cease-fire agreement, fighting between the north and the south continued. Americans, however, paid little heed, their attention riveted instead on impeachment hearings against Nixon, which began in May 1974. Among the charges against Nixon was his secret bombing of Cambodia. On August 8, 1974, Nixon resigned rather than face an impeachment trial.

While the United States was embroiled in Nixon's woes, the North Vietnamese and the Viet Cong waged heavy attacks on South Vietnam. America offered no help to its former war partner. The communist Khmer Rouge seized control of Cambodia on April 16, 1975. Gerald Ford, who became president when Nixon resigned, announced that, in America's eyes, the Vietnam War was over. Two weeks later, North Vietnamese forces captured Saigon and claimed victory over South Vietnam. North Vietnamese Colonel Bui Tin proclaimed the victory "a moment of joy" for all Vietnamese. "Only the Americans have been beaten," he declared.

American military personnel still in Saigon evacuated the remaining U.S. citizens as the city fell. In the chaos, a helicopter crashed, carrying the last two American soldiers to their death.

TImeLIne

Sunday, June 13, 1971
The New York Times prints the first of a ten-part series on the Pentagon Papers.

Monday, June 14
The New York Times prints the second of a ten-part series on the Pentagon Papers.

U.S. Attorney General John Mitchell sends a telegram to *Times* publisher Arthur Ochs Sulzberger to stop publishing the papers and to turn over all top secret material.

The *Times* "respectfully declines" to stop printing the series.

Tuesday, June 15
The New York Times prints the third of a ten-part series on the Pentagon Papers.

Mitchell files suit in U.S. District Court in New York against the *Times*.

District Court Judge Murray Gurfein issues a temporary injunction to stop the *Times* from further publication.

Friday, June 18
Hearing on *The New York Times* publication of the Pentagon Papers is held in U.S. District Court in New York.

The *Washington Post* publishes the first of its articles on the Pentagon Papers.

Assistant Attorney General William Rehnquist warns the *Post* to stop publishing the papers, a warning which the *Post* "respectfully declines" to obey.

The U.S. government files suit in U.S. District Court in Washington, D.C., against the *Post*.

Judge Gerhard Gesell denies the government's request for an injunction against the *Post*.

The U.S. Circuit Court of Appeals in Washington, D.C., holds an emergency session to hear the government's appeal of Gesell's ruling.

Saturday, June 19
The U.S. Circuit Court of Appeals issues an early-morning ruling overturning Gesell's ruling in the *Washington Post* case and orders a hearing in U.S. District Court to be held June 21. The court orders the *Post* to cease publication of the papers beginning on Sunday.

The *Washington Post* publishes the second of its articles on the Pentagon Papers.

Judge Gurfein denies the government's request for an injunction against the *Times.*

The government appeals Gurfein's ruling to the U.S. Circuit Court of Appeals in New York. The court grants the government's request for a temporary injunction to stop the *Times* from publishing further Pentagon Papers documents.

Monday, June 21
The U.S. District Court in Washington, D.C., holds a hearing on the *Post* case. Judge Gesell again denies the government's request for an injunction against the *Post.*

The government once again appeals Gesell's ruling to the U.S. Circuit Court, which grants an extension of the injunction against the *Post.*

Tuesday, June 22
The U.S. Circuit Court of Appeals in New York holds a hearing on *The New York Times* case.

The U.S. Circuit Court of Appeals in Washington, D.C., holds a hearing on the *Washington Post* case.

Wednesday, June 23
The Circuit Court of Appeals in New York rules against *The New York Times* and orders the case to be heard again in U.S. District Court to determine which documents should not be published.

The Circuit Court of Appeals in Washington, D.C., upholds Gesell's decision in favor of the *Washington Post.*

Thursday, June 24
The government requests that the *Post* case be sent back to U.S. District Court to determine which documents should not be published. The request is denied by the U.S. Circuit Court of Appeals.

The New York Times appeals the U.S. Circuit Court of Appeals decision to the U.S. Supreme Court.

The government appeals the *Washington Post* decision to the U.S. Supreme Court.

The Supreme Court agrees to hear the two cases involving the Pentagon Papers. It continues the injunctions against both newspapers until a decision has been issued.

Saturday, June 26
Briefs are due in the two cases.

The Supreme Court hears oral arguments in both cases.

Monday, June 28
The Nixon administration delivers the Pentagon Papers to Congress.

Daniel Ellsberg surrenders to federal agents and is charged with six counts of espionage, six counts of theft, and one count of conspiracy in the Pentagon Papers case.

Tuesday, June 29
Senator Mike Gravel enters his copy of the Pentagon Papers into the Congressional Record.

Wednesday, June 30
U.S. Supreme Court issues decision in favor of the two newspapers, allowing them to continue publishing the Pentagon Papers.

First week in July
The New York Times publishes the remaining seven parts of its series on the Pentagon Papers.

The *Washington Post* publishes a four-day series of articles on the Pentagon Papers.

August 1971
The New York Times version of the Pentagon Papers is published in book form by Bantam Books. It includes a small number of documents, the *Times* articles on the subject, analyses, and the Supreme Court decision.

September 27, 1971
The U.S. government publishes its unclassified version of the Pentagon Papers.

October 22, 1971
Beacon Press publishes the Mike Gravel version of the Pentagon Papers.

1972
The New York Times wins the Pulitzer Prize for Public Service for publishing the Pentagon Papers.

May 11, 1973
U.S. District Court Judge William M. Byrne Jr. throws out the case against Daniel Ellsberg and Anthony J. Russo Jr., citing governmental abuses.

NOTES

Introduction
p. 7, par. 4, *Washington Post*, June 17, 1971.
http://www.washingtonpost.com/wp-srv/inatl/longterm/flash/july/
edit71.htm (Accessed April 5, 2004.)

Chapter 1
p. 9, par. 1–2, "Episode 11: Vietnam," *CNN Perspectives Series*, June
1996. http://www.cnn.com/SPECIALS/cold.war/episodes/11/
interviews/mcnamara (Accessed April 5, 2004.)
p. 12, par. 3, Robert S. McNamara, *Oral History Interview I* by Walt W.
Rostow, January 8, 1975, Internet copy, LBJ Library.
http://www.lbjlib.utexas.edu/johnson/archives.hom/oralhistory.hom/
McNamaraR/McNamara1.PDF (Accessed April 5, 2004.)
p. 12, par. 6–p. 13, par. 2, McNamara, *Oral History Interview I* by Rostow.
David Rudenstine. *The Day the Presses Stopped*. Berkeley: University
of California Press, 1996.

Chapter 2
p. 15, par. 1, Richard Nixon, "Inaugural Address," January 20, 1969,
The American Presidency Project. John Woolley and Gerhard Peters,
University of California, Berkeley.
http://www.presidency.ucsb.edu/docs/inaugurals/nixon1.php
(Accessed April 5, 2004.)
p. 16, par. 4, Daniel Ellsberg, interview by Harry Kreisler, *Reflections
on the Vietnam War: Conversations with Daniel Ellsberg*, July 29,
1998. Connecting Students to the World: Institute of International
Studies, University of California, Berkeley, May 1999.
http://globetrotter.berkeley.edu/people/Ellsberg/ellsberg98-6.html.
(Accessed April 5, 2004.)
p. 17, par. 2, Ellsberg, interview by Kreisler. *Reflections on the
Vietnam War*.
p. 17, par. 3, Ibid.

p. 17, par. 3, Anthony Joseph Russo. "The Pentagon Papers."
http://www.pentagonpaperstrusso.com/summary1.htm
(Accessed April 5, 2004.)

p. 17, par. 4–p. 18, par. 1, David Rudenstine, *The Day the Presses Stopped*. Berkeley: University of California Press, 1996.

p. 18, par. 2, Daniel Ellsberg. *Secrets: A Memoir of Vietnam and the Pentagon Papers*. New York: Viking, 2002.

p. 18, par. 3, Russo. "The Pentagon Papers."

p. 18, par. 5–p. 20, par. 3, Rudenstine. *The Day the Presses Stopped*.

p. 20, par. 1, "The Pentagon Papers with Daniel Ellsberg," washingtonpost.com, October 15, 2002.
http://discuss.washingtonpost.com/
wp-srv/zforum/02/sp_book_ellsberg101502.htm
(Accessed May 26, 2004.)

p. 20, par. 3, Ellsberg. *Secrets: A Memoir of Vietnam and the Pentagon Papers*.

p. 20, par. 5–p. 21, par. 1, Ellsberg. interview by Kreisler, *Reflections on the Vietnam War*.

p. 22, par. 1, "Pentagon Papers" with Brooke Gladstone, *On the Media*, National Public Radio, July 14, 2001.
http://www.wnyc.org/onthemedia/transcripts/
transcripts_071401_pentagon.html (Accessed April 5, 2004.)

p. 22, par. 2, Rudenstine. *The Day the Presses Stopped*.

Chapter 3

p. 24, par. 1–2, *Near v. State of Minnesota ex rel. Olson*, 283 U.S. 697 (1931).

p. 24, par. 3, R. J. Brown. "Colonial America Newspapers," The History Buff. http://www.historybuff.com/library/
refcolonial.html (Accessed April 5, 2004.)

p. 25, par. 3, "History of Press Freedom," Copley First Amendment Center, Dec. 17, 2002.
http://www.illinoisfirstamendmentcenter.com/Main.asp?
SectionID=27&SubSectionID=27&ArticleID=91
(Accessed April 5, 2004.)

p. 25, par. 7–p. 26, par. 1, Jan Huisman, "An Outline of American Government, Fundamentals of American Government," for *From Revolution to Reconstruction—an .HTML project*, March 6, 2003.
http://odur.let.rug.nl/~usa/GOV/ch7_p6.htm
(Accessed April 5, 2004.)

p. 26, par. 3, Derrick Penner. "The Fourth Estate," *UBC Journalism Review, Thunderbird Online Magazine* (The School of Journalism, University of British Columbia) 4, no. 4 (April 2002).
http://www.journalism.ubc.ca/thunderbird/2001-02/april/
opposition. html (Accessed April 5, 2004.)

p. 26, par. 4, James C. Goodale. "The First Amendment and Freedom of the Press," *USIA Electronic Journal* 2, no. 1 (February 1997). http://usinfo.state.gov/journals/itdhr/0297/ijde/goodale.htm (Accessed April 5, 2004.)

p. 27, par. 5, Senate Commission on Protecting and Reducing Government Secrecy, *Secrecy: A Brief Account of the American Experience*, 1997, Senate Document 105-2.

p. 28, par. 1–3, *Schenck v. United States*, 249 US 47 (1919).

p. 29, par. 1, *Secrecy: A Brief Account of the American Experience*.

p. 29, par. 6–p.30, par. 1, Ibid.

p. 30, par. 2, *The New York Times*, June 25, 1957. Cited in *Secrecy: A Brief Account of the American Experience*.

p. 31, par. 1–p. 33, par. 1, *Near v. State of Minnesota ex rel. Olson*, 283 U.S. 697 (1931).

p. 33, par. 2–3, Anthony Lewis. *Make No Law: The Sullivan Case and the First Amendment*. New York: Random House, 1991.

p. 33, par. 4–p. 34, par. 3, *New York Times Co. v. Sullivan*, 376 U.S. 254 (1964).

Chapter 4

p. 35, par. 2–4, James Goodale, interview, *Frontline*, PBS, 1999. http://www.pbs.org/wgbh/pages/frontline/smoke/interviews/goodale. html (Accessed April 5, 2004.)

p. 36, par. 2–3, David Rudenstine. *The Day the Presses Stopped*. Berkeley: University of California Press, 1996.

p. 36, par.–p. 37, par. 5, *The New York Times*, June 13, 1971, p. 1.

p. 37, par. 7, *The New York Times*, June 13, 1971, p. 1.

pp. 38–40, *The Pentagon Papers, Gravel Edition*. Boston: Beacon Press, 1971.

p. 41, par. 1–p. 42, par. 4, Richard M. Nixon, tapes, June 13, 1971, recorded from Nixon Library Materials at NARA, College Park, on May 30, 2001. White House Tape WHT-5, Cassette 825, Conversation 5-50; Transcribed at National Security Archive, May 31, 2001, by Eddie Meadows. http://www.gwu.edu/~nsarchiv/NSAEBB/NSAEBB48/nixon.html (Accessed April 5, 2004.)

p. 42, par. 6–p. 43, par. 3, Nixon tapes, June 14, 1971.

p. 44, par. 1, H. R. Haldeman. *The Haldeman Diaries*. New York: Berkeley Books, 1995.

p. 44, par. 2–p. 45, par. 3, Nixon tapes, June 14, 1971.

p. 45, par. 4, *The New York Times*, June 15, 1971. http://www.nytimes.com/books/97/04/13/reviews/papers-mitchell.html (Accessed April 5, 2004.)

p. 46, par. 1, *The New York Times*, June 15, 1971.

p. 46, par. 4, Nixon tapes, June 15, 1971.

p. 46, par. 5, *The New York Times*, June 16, 1996. http://www.nytimes.com/books/97/04/13/reviews/ papers-secret.html (Accessed April 5, 2004.)

p. 47, par. 1, *ABC Evening News*, Television News Archive, Vanderbilt University, June 15, 1971. http://tvnews.vanderbilt.edu/TV-NewsSearch (Accessed April 5, 2004.)

p. 47, par. 2, Nixon tapes, June 15, 1971.

p. 47, par. 3, Richard M. Nixon. *The Memoirs of Richard Nixon*. New York: Grosset & Dunlap, 1978.

p. 48, par. 2, David Rudenstine. *The Day the Presses Stopped*.

p. 49, par. 3, Philip B. Kurland and Gerhard Casper, eds. "*New York Times* v. *United States (1971),*" *Landmark Briefs and Arguments*, 71. Arlington, Virginia: University Publications of America Inc., 1975.

p. 49, par. 4–p. 50, par. 1, The National Security Archive, "Secrets, Lies and Audiotapes." http://www.gwu.edu/~nsarchiv/NSAEBB/NSAEBB48/nixon.html (Accessed April 5, 2004.)

p. 50, par. 3–p. 51, par. 1, The National Security Archive, "Secrets, Lies and Audiotapes."

p. 51, par. 3–5, Rudenstine. *The Day the Presses Stopped*.

p. 51, par. 7–p. 52, par. 1, Kurland and Casper, *Landmark Briefs and Arguments*.

Chapter 5

p. 53, par. 1–3, Katharine Graham. *Personal History*. New York: Vintage Books, 1997.

p. 54, par. 1, Washington Post, June 17, 1971. http://www.washington post.com/wp-srv/inatl/longterm/flash/july/ edit71.htm (Accessed April 5, 2004.)

p. 54, par. 5–p. 55, par. 2, Graham. *Personal History*.

p. 55, par. 3, *The New York Times*, June 23, 1972, p. 23, col. 6. Cited by James Goodale in "News Media and the Law," *New York Law Journal*, May 26, 1977.

p. 55, par. 4, "Pentagon Papers: The Secret War," *Time*, June 28, 1971. http://www.cnn.com/ALLPOLITICS/1996/analysis/back.time/ 9606/28/index.shtml (Accessed April 6, 2004.)

p. 56, par. 2, David Rudenstine. *The Day the Presses Stopped*.

p. 56, par. 3–p. 57, par. 1, Graham, *Personal History*.

p. 57, par. 2–4, Rudenstine. *The Day the Presses Stopped*.

p. 57, par. 5–p. 58, par. 2, Philip B. Kurland and Gerhard Casper, eds. *"New York Times* v. *United States (1971),"* Landmark Briefs and Arguments, 71. Arlington, Virginia: University Publications of America Inc., 1975.

p. 58, par. 5–6, Rudenstine. *The Day the Presses Stopped.*

p. 59, par. 1, Kurland and Casper. *Landmark Briefs and Arguments.*

p. 59, par. 2, Justice Harry Blackmun dissent, *New York Times Co.* v. *United States*, 403 U.S. 713 (1971).

p. 59, par. 3, Kurland and Casper. *Landmark Briefs and Arguments.*

p. 59, par. 6, *NBC Evening News*, Television News Archive, Vanderbilt University, June 15, 1971. http://tvnews.vanderbilt.edu/TV-NewsSearch. Accessed April 6, 2004.

p. 60, par. 1, *ABC Evening News*, Television News Archive, Vanderbilt University, June 17, 1971. http://tvnews.vanderbilt.edu/TV-NewsSearch (Accessed April 6, 2004.)

p. 60, par. 3, "Pentagon Papers: The Secret War," *Time*, June 28, 1971.

p. 60, par. 5–6, *ABC Evening News*, Television News Archive, Vanderbilt University, June 15, 1971. http://tvnews.vanderbilt.edu/TV-NewsSearch (Accessed April 6, 2004.)

p. 61, par. 4, *CBS Evening News*, Television News Archive, Vanderbilt University, June 22, 1971. http://tvnews.vanderbilt.edu/TV-NewsSearch (Accessed April 6, 2004.)

p. 61, par. 5–p. 62, par. 1, *NBC Evening News*, Television News Archive, Vanderbilt University, June 16, 1971. http://tvnews.vanderbilt.edu/TV-NewsSearch (Accessed April 6, 2004.)

p. 62, par. 2 (first half), "High School Students' E-Mail Exchange with Daniel Ellsberg," Connecting Students to the World: Institute of International Studies, University of California Berkeley, May 1999. http://globetrotter.berkeley.edu/people/Ellsberg/ells.QA99.leak.html (Accessed April 6, 2004.)

p. 62, par. 2 ("clean air"), "Pentagon Papers" with Brooke Gladstone, *On the Media*, National Public Radio, July 14, 2001. http://www.wnyc.org/onthemedia/transcripts/ transcripts_071401_pentagon.html (Accessed April 6, 2004.)

p. 62, par. 2 (last quote), *CBS Evening News*, Television News Archive, Vanderbilt University, June 23, 1971.

http://tvnews.vanderbilt.edu/TV-NewsSearch
(Accessed April 6, 2004.)

Chapter 6

p. 64, par. 5–p. 65, par. 1, David Rudenstine. *The Day the Presses Stopped.* Berkeley: University of California Press, 1996.

p. 66, par. 4–p. 67, par. 6, Philip B. Kurland and Gerhard Casper, eds. *"New York Times* v. *United States (1971),"* Landmark Briefs and Arguments, 71. Arlington, Virginia: University Publications of America Inc., 1975.

pp. 68–69 Iowa Court Information System http://www.judicial.state.ia.us/students/6 (Accessed Nov. 3, 2003.) The Supreme Court Historical Society http://www.supremecourthistory.org (Accessed Nov. 3, 2003.) Administrative Office of the U.S. Courts http://www.uscourts.gov (Accessed Nov. 3, 2003.)

p. 70, par. 1–5, Kurland and Casper, eds. *"New York Times* v. *United States (1971),"* Landmark Briefs and Arguments, 71.

p. 73, par. 4–p. 75, par. 6, Kurland and Casper, eds. *Landmark Briefs and Arguments.*

p. 76, par. 1, Rudenstine. *The Day the Presses Stopped.*

p. 76, par. 2–p. 78, par. 7, Kurland and Casper, eds. *Landmark Briefs and Arguments.*

p. 78, par. 9–p. 80, par. 5, Kurland and Casper, eds. *Landmark Briefs and Arguments.*

P. 80, par. 7–p. 81, par. 6, Kurland and Casper, eds. *Landmark Briefs and Arguments.*

p. 81, par. 7, Rudenstine. *The Day the Presses Stopped.*

Chapter 7

p. 83, par. 5–p. 84, par. 2, David Rudenstine, *The Day the Presses Stopped.* Berkeley: University of California Press, 1996.

p. 87, par. 4–p. 88, par. 4, Justice Hugo Black concurring opinion, *New York Times Co.* v. *United States,* 403 U.S. 713 (1971).

p. 88, par. 5–6, Justice William O. Douglas concurring opinion, *New York Times Co.* v. *United States,* 403 U.S. 713 (1971).

p. 88, par. 7–p. 89, par. 1, Justice William J. Brennan concurring opinion, *New York Times Co.* v. *United States,* 403 U.S. 713 (1971).

p. 89, par. 2–7, Justice Potter Stewart concurring opinion, *New York Times Co.* v. *United States,* 403 U.S. 713 (1971).

p. 89, par. 8–p. 90, par. 2, Justice Byron White concurring opinion, *New York Times Co.* v. *United States,* 403 U.S. 713 (1971).

p. 90, par. 3–4, Justice Thurgood Marshall concurring opinion,

New York Times Co. v. United States, 403 U.S. 713 (1971).
p. 90, par. 5–p. 91, par. 2, Chief Justice Warren Burger dissent,
New York Times Co. v. United States, 403 U.S. 713 (1971).
p. 90, par. 3–4, Justice John Marshall Harlan dissent, *New York
Times Co. v. United States*, 403 U.S. 713 (1971).
p. 90, par. 5, Justice Harry Blackmun dissent, *New York Times
Co. v. United States*, 403 U.S. 713 (1971).

Chapter 8

p. 92, par. 1–2, *The New York Times*, July 1, 1971.
http://www.nytimes.com/books/97/04/13/reviews/papers-final.html
(Accessed April 6, 2004.)
p. 92, par. 3, *Washington Post*, July 1, 1971.
http://www.washingtonpost.com/wp-srv/inatl/longterm/flash/july/pent71.htm
(Accessed April 6, 2004.)
p. 92, par. 4, David Rudenstine. *The Day the Presses Stopped.*
Berkeley: University of California Press, 1996.
p. 93, par. 6, Rudenstine. *The Day the Presses Stopped.*
p. 94, par. 2, Fairbanks *Daily News-Miner*, June 7, 2001.
http://peninsulaclarion.com/stories/060701/ala_060701ala0130001.
shtml (Accessed April 6, 2004.)
p. 94, par. 3, "A courageous press confronts a deceptive government,"
UU World Magazine, Unitarian Universalist Association,
September/October 2001, adapted from *The Premise and the
Promise: The Story of the Unitarian Universalist Association*, by
Warren R. Ross, published by Skinner House Books, 2001.
http://www.uua.org/world/2001/04/lookingback.html
(Accessed April 6, 2004.)
p. 95, par. 1, "Mike Gravel," National Initiative for Democracy.
http://ni4d.us/people/gravel2.htm. Accessed April 6, 2004.
p. 95, par. 2, Susan Wilson, Brief History of Beacon Press, Boston:
Beacon Press, 2003. www.beacon.org/chapbook/03.bpo316.pdf
(Accessed April 6, 2004.)
p. 95, par. 3–6, Deborah Weiner, ed., "Gobin Stair and Rev. Robert
West Recount UUA/Beacon Press Publication of 'The Pentagon
Papers,'" *UUs and the News*, October 17, 2002, Unitarian
Universalist Association http://www.uua.org/news/2002/civil/
pentagon.html (Accessed April 6, 2004.)
p. 96, par. 1, The Rev. Dr. Raymond Hopkins, in interview with the
author, December 5, 2003.
p. 96, par. 3, Weiner, ed., "Gobin Stair and Rev. Robert West
recount UUA/Beacon Press Publication of 'The Pentagon Papers.'"
p. 96, par. 4, *Gravel v. United States*, 408 U.S. 606 (1972).

p. 97, par. 2–3, The Rev. Dr. Raymond Hopkins.

p. 97, par. 4–5, "Voices from the Past: Defending the Pentagon Papers" *UU World Magazine*, Unitarian Universalist Association, September 15, 1971.
http://www.uua.org/world/2001/04/lookingback.html (Accessed April 6, 2004.)

p. 98, par.1–2, Rudenstine. *The Day the Presses Stopped*.

p. 98, par. 5–p. 99, par. 2, Stanley I. Kutler, ed. *Abuse of Power: The New Nixon Tapes*. New York: The Free Press, 2001.

p. 98, par. 4, Richard M. Nixon. *The Memoirs of Richard Nixon*. New York: Grosset & Dunlap, 1978.

p. 100, par. 1, Daniel Ellsberg, "Cold War Chat: Daniel Ellsberg, Anti-war Activist," with Bruce Kennedy, *CNN Perspectives Series*, January 10, 1999.
http://www.cnn.com/SPECIALS/cold.war/guides/debate/chats/ellsberg (Accessed April 6, 2004.)

p. 100, par. 3–p. 101, par. 1, The New York Times, May 12, 1973.
http://www.nytimes.com/learning/general/onthisday/big/0511.html (Accessed April 6, 2004.)

p. 101, par. 2, Nixon. *The Memoirs of Richard Nixon*.

p. 103, par. 2, Daniel Ellsberg, "Cold War Chat: Daniel Ellsberg, Anti-war Activist," with Bruce Kennedy, *CNN Perspectives Series*, January 10, 1999.
http://www.cnn.com/SPECIALS/cold.war/guides/debate/chats/ellsberg (Accessed April 6, 2004.)

p. 103, par. 3, *Hustler Magazine, Inc.* v. *Falwell*, 485 U.S. 46 (1988).

p. 104, par. 1, Howard Morland. "The H-bomb secret: How we got it-why we're telling it, *The Progressive*, November 1979.
http://www.progressive.org/pdf/1179.pdf (Accessed April 6, 2004.)

p. 104, par. 2, Samuel H. Day. *Crossing the Line: From Editor to Activist to Inmate: A Writer's Journey*. Minneapolis: Fortress Press, 1991.

p. 105, par. 4, Katharine Graham. *Personal History*. New York: Vintage Books, 1997.

p. 105, par. 5–p. 106, par. 1, USA Patriot Act, HR3162, October 24, 2001.

p. 106, par. 1, *Casper Star-Tribune*, January 23, 2003.
http://www.prisonplanet.com/news_alert_012303_patriot.html (Accessed April 5, 2004.)

p. 106, par. 2–3, John Podesta, "Remarks at Princeton University, Center for American Progress," March 10, 2004.
http://www.americanprogress.org/site/pp.asp?c=biJRJ8OVF&b=36889 (Accessed April 5, 2004.)

p. 107, par. 1, *Washington Post*, December 7, 2001, p. A40.

p. 107, par. 2, Matthew Silverman, "National Security and the First Amendment: A Judicial Role in Maximizing Public Access to Information." http://www.law.indiana.edu/ilj/v78/no3/silverman.pdf (Accessed April 5, 2004.)

p. 107, par. 2, *Detroit Free Press, et al.* v. *John Ashcroft, et al.*, 0291P (6th Cir. 2002).

p. 107, par. 3 (Ashcroft), John Ashcroft to Rep. J. Dennis Hastert, October 15, 2002. http://www.fas.org/sgp/othergov/dojleaks.html (Accessed April 6, 2004.)

p. 107, par. 3 (Bush)–p. 108, par. 1, John W. Dean, "Bush's Unofficial Official Secrets Act: How the Justice Department Has Pushed to Criminalize The Disclosure of Non-Security Related Government Information," September 26, 2003. http://writ.news.findlaw.com/dean/20030926.html (Accessed April 5, 2004.)

p. 108, par. 2, Senate Commission on Protecting and Reducing Government Secrecy, Secrecy: A Brief Account of the American Experience, 1997, Senate Document 105-2.

p. 108, par. 3–5, *Washington Post*, Feb. 15, 1989, A25. Cited in *Secrecy: A Brief Account of the American Experience.*

p. 109, par. 1–2, Cynthia Fuchs. "The Pentagon Papers: You Can't Escape." *Pop Matters Television*, March 9, 2003. http://www.popmatters.com/tv/reviews/p/pentagon-papers.shtml (Accessed April 6, 2004.)

p. 109, par. 3–6, Sanford Ungar, "Individuals and the Security Services," at Security Services in Civil Society: Oversight and Accountability International Conference, June 30–July 2, 1995, Warsaw. http://www.hfhrpol.waw.pl/Secserv/conf_rept/indiv.html (Accessed April 6, 2004.)

Appendix

p. 110, par. 2, William A. McGeveran Jr., ed. dir. *The World Almanac and Book of Facts: 2002.* New York: World Almanac Books, 2002.

p. 110, par. 2, Don Poss, ed. "Vietnam Veterans' War Stories," 1997. http://www.war-stories.com/wall-search-1.htm (Accessed April 6, 2004.)

p. 110, par. 3, Kaushik Basu. "A Vietnam Diary." Cornell University. http://www.people.cornell.edu/pages/kb40/9.3.01.PDF (Accessed May 28, 2004.)

p. 110, par. 3–p. 111, par. 1, "YSN sponsored conference advances knowledge of Vietnam's toxic legacy," Yale University School of Nursing, 2001.

http://www.nursing.yale.edu/news/vwsymposium.html
(Accessed April 6, 2004.)

p. 111, par. 2, Hang Pham, "ICE Case Studies: Vietnam," Inventory of
Conflict and Environment, Summer 1997.
http://www.american.edu/TED/ice/vietnam.htm
(Accessed April 6, 2004.)

p. 111, par. 6–7, *The American Experience: Vietnam Online*, PBS,
WGBH, Boston. http://www.pbs.org/wgbh/amex/vietnam/time/
tl1-noframes.html (Accessed April 6, 2004.)

p. 111, par. 8; p. 112, par. 2, John Prados, "JFK and the Diem Coup,"
November 5, 2003, National Security Archive.
http://www.gwu.edu/~nsarchiv/NSAEBB/NSAEBB101/index.htm
(Accessed April 6, 2004.)

p. 114, par. 4, *The American Experience: Vietnam Online*, PBS.

p. 115, par. 2–3, ibid.

FurTHer inFormaTion

BOOKS

Campbell, Geoffrey A. *The Pentagon Papers: National Security Versus the Public's Right to Know* (Words That Changed History). San Diego: Lucent Books, 2000.

Cornelius, Kay. *The Supreme Court* (Your Government: How It Works). Broomall, PA: Chelsea House Publishers, 2000.

Denenberg, Barry. *Voices from Vietnam*. New York: Scholastic, 1995.

Feinberg, Barbara Silberdick. *Watergate: Scandal in the White House* (Twentieth Century American History Series). New York: Franklin Watts, 1990.

Heath, David, and Charlotte Wilcox. *The Supreme Court of the United States* (American Civics). Mankato, MN: Bridgestone Books, 1999.

Herda, D. J. New York Times *v.* United States: *National Security and Censorship* (Landmark Supreme Court Cases). Berkeley Heights, NJ: Enslow Publishers, 1994.

Levert, Suzanne. *The Supreme Court*. New York: Benchmark Books, 2002.

Netzley, Patricia D. *Issues in Censorship* (Contemporary Issues). San Diego: Lucent Books, 2000.

Patrick, John J. *The Supreme Court of the United States: A Student Companion* (Oxford Student Companions to American Government), 2nd ed. New York: Oxford University Press Children's Books, 2002.

Sanders, Mark C. *Supreme Court* (American Government Today Series). Austin, TX: Raintree/Steck-Vaughn Publishers, 2001.

Stay, Byron L., ed. *Censorship:* (Opposing Viewpoints Series). Farmington Hills, MI: Greenhaven Press, 1997.

Zeinert, Karen. *Free Speech: From Newspapers to Music Lyrics* (Issues in Focus). Berkeley Heights, NJ: Enslow Publishers, 1995.

AUDIO
Cowan, Geoffrey, and Leroy Aarons. *Top Secret: The Battle for the Pentagon Papers* (Audio Theatre Series). Los Angeles: L.A. Theatre Works, 1992.

Nixon, Richard. *The President Calling* (American RadioWorks) http://www.americanradioworks.org/features/prestapes/index.html.

The Pentagon Papers (audiotape of Supreme Court oral arguments and Nixon tapes) http://www.gwu.edu/~nsarchiv/NSAEBB/NSAEBB48

WEB SITES
"ABC Evening News," Television News Archive. http://www.vanderbilt.edu/TV-NewsSearch

The American Experience: Vietnam Online, PBS, WGBH, Boston http://www.pbs.org/wgbh/amex/vietnam/time/tl1-noframes.html

Ashcroft, John. To Rep. J. Dennis Hastert, October 15, 2002 http://www.fas.org/sgp/othergov/dojleaks.html

Brown, R.J. "Colonial American Newspapers,"
The History Buff.
http://www.historybuff.com/library/refcolonial.html

Citrine, Charlie. *Watergate Timeline*
http://www.tropes.com/History/Biography/UnitedStates/Presidents
oftheUnitedStates/NixonRichardMilhous/WatergateTimeline.html

Constitutional Rights Foundation. "First Amendment and the Press"
http://www.crf-usa.org/lessons/right_to_know_guide.htm

Dean, John W. "Bush's Unofficial Official Secrets Act: How the
Justice Department Has Pushed to Criminalize The Disclosure
of Non-Security Related Government Information"
http://writ.news.findlaw.com/dean/20030926.html

Ellsberg, Daniel. "Cold War Chat: Daniel Ellsberg, Anti-war Activist,"
with Bruce Kennedy, *CNN Perspectives Series*, January 10, 1999
http://www.cnn.com/SPECIALS/cold.war/guides/debate/chats/ellsberg

Famous American Trials, "John Peter Zenger Trial," 1735
http://www.law.umkc.edu/faculty/projects/ftrials/zenger/zenger.html

FindLaw, U.S. Supreme Court decisions
http://www.findlaw.com/casecode/supreme.html
Goodale, James, attorney for *The New York Times*
http://www.jamesgoodale.net/pages/1/index.htm

Goodale, James. Interview, *Frontline*, PBS, 1999
http://www.pbs.org/wgbh/pages/frontline/smoke/interviews/goodale.html

Gravel, Mike, *Sen. Edition of the Pentagon Papers*
http://www.beacon.org/notables/pentagonpapers.html

"High School Students' E-Mail Exchange with Daniel Ellsberg,"
Connecting Students to the World: Institute of International Studies,
University of California Berkeley, May 1999
http://globetrotter.berkeley.edu/people/Ellsberg/ells.QA99.leak.html

"History of Press Freedom," Copley First Amendment Center, Dec. 17, 2002
http://www.illinoisfirstamendmentcenter.com/Main.asp?Sect
ionID=27&SubSectionID=27&ArticleID=91

Legal Information Institute, Cornell Law School
http://www.law.cornell.edu

Libel Defense Resource Center, Inc. (now known as Media Law
Resource Center [MLRC]
http://www.ldrc.com/Press_Releases/bull2002-2.html

McNamara, Robert S. *Oral History Interview I* by Walt W. Rostow,
January 8, 1975, Internet Copy, LBJ Library
http://www.lbjlib.utexas.edu/johnson/archives.hom/oralhistory.
hom/ McNamaraR/McNamara1.PDF

"Mike Gravel," National Initiative for Democracy
http://ni4d.us/people/gravel2.htm

The National Security Archive. *The Pentagon Papers*, audiotape of
Supreme Court oral arguments and Nixon tapes
http://www.gwu.edu/~nsarchiv/NSAEBB/NSAEBB48

Nixon, Richard. "Inaugural Address," January 20, 1969, The
American Presidency Project. John Woolley and Gerhard Peters,

———. White House tapes.
http://www.gwu.edu/~nsarchiv/NSAEBB/NSAEBB48/nixon.html

Oyez Project: U.S. Supreme Court Multimedia Web site
http://www.oyez.org/oyez/frontpage

Penner, Derrick. "The Fourth Estate," *UBC Journalism Review,
Thunderbird Online Magazine* (The School of Journalism,
University of British Columbia) 4, no. 4 (April 2002)
http://www.journalism.ubc.ca/thunderbird/archives/2002.04/
opposition.html

"Pentagon Papers" with Brooke Gladstone, *On the Media*, National Public Radio, July 14, 2001
http://www.wnyc.org/onthemedia/
transcripts/transcripts_071401_pentagon. html

"The Pentagon Papers With Daniel Ellsberg," washingtonpost.com archives, October 15, 2002
http://www.washingtonpost.com/wp-srv/liveonline/02/
special/books/sp_books_ellsberg101502.html

Pham, Hang. "ICE Case Studies: Vietnam," Inventory of Conflict and Environment, Summer 1997
http://www.american.edu/TED/ice/vietnam/htm

Podesta, John. "Remarks at Princeton University, Center for American Progress," March 10, 2004
http://www.americanprogress.org/site/pp.asp?c=biJRJ8OVF&b=36889

Poss, Don, ed. "Vietnam Veterans' War Stories," 1997
http://www.war-stories.com/wall-search-1.htm

Prados, John. "JFK and the Diem Coup," November 5, 2003, National Security Archive
http://www.gwu.edu/~nsarchiv/NSAEBB/NSAEBB101/index.htm

Reporters Committee for Freedom of the Press
http://www.rcfp.org

Russo, Anthony Joseph. "The Pentagon Papers"
http://www.pentagonpaperstrusso.com

Smith, Stephen, and Kate Ellis. "White House Tapes: The President Calling," *American RadioWorks*
http://www.americanradioworks.org/features/prestapes/index.html

Starr, Bob. *Studying the Vietnam War Online*
http://www.refstar.com/vietnam/online_study.html

Supreme Court Historical Society
http://www.supremecourthistory.org

Supreme Court of the United States
http://www.supremecourtus.gov

Ungar, Sanford. "Individuals and the Security Services," at Security Services in Civil Society: Oversight and Accountability International Conference, June 30–July 2, 1995, Warsaw
http://www.hfhrpol.waw.pl/Secserv/conf_rept/indiv.html

Vietnam Veterans of America, "The Pentagon Papers" (includes many links to articles, original documents, *The New York Times* and *Washington Post* articles)
http://www.vva.org/pentagon/links/links2.html

Weiner, Deborah, ed. "Gobin Stair and Rev. Robert West recount UUA/Beacon Press Publication of 'The Pentagon Papers,'" *UUs and the News*, October 17, 2002, Unitarian Universalist Association
http://www.uua.org/news/2002/civil/pentagon.html

"YSN sponsored conference advances knowledge of Vietnam's toxic legacy," Yale University School of Nursing, 2001
http://www.nursing.yale.edu/news/vwsymposium.html

All Web sites accessible as of April 6, 2004.

BIBLIOGraPHY

Articles

"A courageous press confronts a deceptive government," *UU World Magazine*, Unitarian Universalist Association, September/October 2001, adapted from *The Premise and the Promise: The Story of the Unitarian Universalist Association*, by Warren R. Ross, published by Skinner House Books, 2001
http://www.uua.org/world/2001/04/lookingback.html

Casper Star-Tribune, January 23, 2003
http://www.prisonplanet.com/news_alert_012303_patriot.html

Fairbanks Daily News-Miner, June 7, 2001
http://peninsulaclarion.com/stories/060701/ala_060701ala0130001.shtml

Hang Pham, "ICE Case Studies: Vietnam," *Inventory of Conflict and Environment*, Summer 1997
http://www.american.edu/TED/ice/vietnam.htm

Morland, Howard. "The H-bomb secret: How we got it—why we're telling it, *The Progressive*, November 1979
http://www.progressive.org/pdf/1179.pdf

The New York Times, June 15, 1971
http://www.nytimes.com/books/97/04/13/reviews/papers-mitchell.html

The New York Times, June 16, 1996
http://www.nytimes.com/books/97/04/13/reviews/papers-secret.html

The New York Times, July 1, 1971
http://www.nytimes.com/books/97/04/13/reviews/papers-final.html

The New York Times, May 12, 1973
http://www.nytimes.com/learning/general/onthisday/big/0511.html

"Pentagon Papers: The Secret War," *Time* magazine, June 28, 1971
http://www.cnn.com/ALLPOLITICS/1996/analysis/back.time/9606/28/index.shtml

Star-Telegram, April 13, 2003
http://www.dfw.com/mld/startelegram/2003/04/13/news/editorial/5624588.htm?1c

"Voices from the past: Defending the Pentagon Papers" *UU World Magazine*, Unitarian Universalist Association, September 15, 1971
http://www.uua.org/world/2001/04/lookingback.html

Washington Post, June 17, 1971
http://www.washingtonpost.com/wp-srv/inatl/longterm/flash/july/edit71.htm

Washington Post, July 1, 1971
http://www.washingtonpost.com/wp-srv/inatl/longterm/flash/july/pent71.htm

All Web sites accessible as of April 6, 2004.

BOOKS

Bernstein, Carl, and Bob Woodward. *All the President's Men.* New York: Simon & Schuster, 1994.

Day, Samuel H. *Crossing the Line: From Editor to Activist to Inmate: A Writer's Journey.* Minneapolis, MN: Fortress Press, 1991.

Ellsberg, Daniel. *Secrets: A Memoir of Vietnam and the Pentagon Papers*. New York: Viking, 2002.

Gelb, Arthur. *City Room*. New York: Putnam Publishing Group, 2003.

Graham, Katharine. *Personal History*. New York: Vintage Books, 1997.

Halberstam, David. *The Best and the Brightest*. New York: Ballantine Books, 1993.

Haldeman, H. R. *The Haldeman Diaries*. New York: Berkeley Books, 1995.

Herring, George C. *America's Longest War: The United States and Vietnam, 1950–1975*. New York: McGraw-Hill, 2001.

Karnow, Stanley. *Vietnam: A History*. New York: Penguin USA, 1997.

Kissinger, Henry. *Years of Upheaval*. Boston: Little, Brown and Co., 1982.

Kurland, Philip B., and Gerhard Casper, eds. *"New York Times v. United States* (1971)," *Landmark Briefs and Arguments*, 71. Arlington, VA: University Publications of America Inc., 1975.

Kutler, Stanley, ed. *Abuse of Power: The New Nixon Tapes*. New York: The Free Press, 2001.

Lewis, Anthony. *Make No Law: The Sullivan Case and the First Amendment*. New York: Random House, 1991.

McGeveran, William A., Jr., ed. dir. *The World Almanac and Book of Facts: 2002*. New York: World Almanac Books, 2002.

McNamara, Robert, with Brian VanDeMark. *In Retrospect: The Tragedy and Lessons of Vietnam*. New York: Times Books/Random House, 1995.

Nixon, Richard M. *The Memoirs of Richard Nixon.* New York: Grosset & Dunlap, 1978.

Rudenstine, David. *The Day the Presses Stopped.* Berkeley: University of California Press, 1996.

Sheehan, Neil. *A Bright Shining Lie: John Paul Vann and America in Vietnam.* New York: Vintage Books, 1989.

———. *The Pentagon Papers as* published by The New York Times. New York: *The New York Times,* 1971.

Ungar, Sanford J. *The Papers & The Papers: An Account of the Legal and Political Battle over the Pentagon Papers.* New York: Dutton, 1972.

Wells, Tom. *Wild Man: The Life and Times of Daniel Ellsberg.* New York: Palgrave, 2001.

Wilson, Susan. *Brief History of Beacon Press,* Boston: Beacon Press, 2003 www.beacon.org/chapbook/03.bpo316.pdf

(Web sites accessed April 6, 2004.)

Statutes/Court Cases/Documents

Detroit Free Press, et al. v. *John Ashcroft, et al.* , 0291P F. (6th Cir. 2002).

Espionage Act of 1917.

Gravel v. *United States,* 408 U.S. 606 (1972).

Hustler Magazine, Inc. v. *Falwell,* 485 U.S. 46 (1988).

Near v. *State of Minnesota ex rel. Olson,* 283 U.S. 697 (1931).

New York Times Co. v. *Sullivan,* 376 U.S. 254 (1964).

New York Times Co. v. *United States,* 403 U.S. 713 (1971).

Sedition Act of 1798.

U.S. Congress. Senate Commission on Protecting and Reducing Government Secrecy, *Secrecy: A Brief Account of the American Experience,* 1997, Senate Document 105-2.

USA Patriot Act, HR3162. Public Law 107-56, October 26, 2001.

index

Page numbers in **boldface** are illustrations, tables, and charts

about the author

SUSAN DUDLEY GOLD has written more than three dozen books for middle-school and high-school students on a variety of topics, including American history, health issues, law, and space. Her most recent works for Benchmark Books are *Gun Control* in the Open for Debate series, and *Roe v. Wade: A Woman's Choice?*, *Brown v. Board of Education: Separate but Equal?*, and *The Pentagon Papers: National Security or the Right to Know*—all in the Supreme Court Milestones series. She is currently working on three more books about Supreme Court cases.

Susan Gold has also written several books on Maine history. Among her many careers in journalism are stints as a reporter for a daily newspaper, managing editor of two statewide business magazines, and freelance writer for several regional publications. She and her husband, John Gold, own and operate a Web design and publishing business. Susan has received numerous awards for her writing and design work. In 2001 she received a Jefferson Award for community service in recognition of her work with a support group for people with chronic pain, which she founded in 1993. Susan and her husband, also a children's book author, live in Maine. They have one son, Samuel.

ETHELBERT B. CRAWFORD PUBLIC LIBRARY
393 BROADWAY, MONTICELLO, NY 12701